I hope you find inspiration along the way as you take this journey with me —

Ellen Rubin

11/2012

Cinderella is Still Dancing

8 CHOICES THAT CAN IMPROVE YOUR LIFE

ELLEN KIRTON

authorHOUSE®

AuthorHouse™
1663 Liberty Drive
Bloomington, IN 47403
www.authorhouse.com
Phone: 1-800-839-8640

First published by AuthorHouse 9/8/2009

ISBN: 978-1-4490-0925-0 (e)
ISBN: 978-1-4490-0924-3 (sc)

Library of Congress Control Number: 2009907349

Printed in the United States of America
Bloomington, Indiana

This book is printed on acid-free paper.

Edited by Diane Sears, DiVerse Media, www.di-verse-media.com
Cover illustration and interior illustrations by Melo Dominguez, www.mrocla.com

To order the book, please visit www.AuthorHouse.com

The author offers discounts on this book when ordered in quantity. Please contact info@ellenkirton.com.

Some of the proceeds from this book are being donated to New Beginnings for Women & Children, www.nbwctuscon.org.

Dedication

This book is dedicated to my daughter Christina and granddaughter Zoie for being the best successes in my life! As Christina conquered her cancer in such a courageous way to be there for Zoie, I was truly inspired and proud.

Also Audrey Watson, my best friend, who has loved me during and in spite of all the transitions in my life. It is priceless to have a friend's unconditional love.

Lastly, to Pam Hamilton, who left her legacy of art to brighten every day for me and inspired me to leave this legacy.

Acknowledgments

I'd like to acknowledge the contributions in my life that led to this book:

- In memory of my mother, Dorothy Brown, now at peace.

- My siblings, Eileen Forte, Karen Martin, Mary Barlow and Tom Moonan, who mean so very much to me.

- My daughter Christina and granddaughter Zoie, of whom I am so proud. They have supported me on every step of this journey!

- My best friend Audrey Watson, always by my side encouraging me and making me laugh in spite of myself.

- My special friend Pam Hamilton, a gifted artist taken too early by breast cancer. She inspired me to leave a legacy such as she did with her incredible art.

- Lola Kakes, my friend and business partner ... she truly lives the life of helping others and has dedicated herself not only to family but also to the small business community across the country.

- Jane Burch, executive director of New Beginnings for Women & Children. Jane is an incredible leader of this organization, and if there had been a resource like this for my family when I was growing up, many things could have been far different in a positive way.

- My editor, Diane Sears, who taught me a whole different way of writing that I hope readers really enjoy. She made this journey a memorable one and she has a wonderful knack for never making you feel inadequate along the way. Instead, she is always encouraging and brilliant at what she does.

Contents

Foreword

Producing a book that grabs you from the opening and carries you on a journey is nothing short of several miracles. Really, how much more can a reader ask for than the achievement strategies for life that Ellen presents in this biographical story that offers personal lessons for everyone?

In the opening chapter, I was struck by her environment and what it took to exist in a home and life full of abuse. In the middle of the book, the hardships and successes Ellen experienced on several levels had me questioning whether I could have accomplished the same. And with each chapter of Ellen's story, and each lesson she learned from people along the way, I became more intrigued.

From the moment I saw Ellen beginning to grow in her story, I knew she was a person of many windows. What I discovered – what I hope others discover – is that she shines the light on a way to find the hidden paths that help us all. This is a story that marches us straight to the goal of better self-vision.

Ellen, thanks for sharing. I wish you showers – no, make that torrential downpours – of love, light and everything good.

Greg Winston,

Sales consultant and motivational speaker

www.GregWinston.com

June 2009

A Special Note

New Beginnings for Women and Children is about *people;* people who need help, people who give help and people who support that help. It may sound simplistic, but it really isn't. The mission of a human service agency such as ours depends on people's understanding of and compassion for other people – and their willingness to act on this understanding.

No matter how many people we serve, every action becomes personal and individualized. One life can be changed by the caring strength of a counselor. One person at a time, one contribution at a time makes it possible for the agency to survive financially. One person can be an ambassador to the community and have an impact that no one is able to know for certain.

Ellen Kirton has been one of these people for New Beginnings for Women & Children. She will never know how many others she has helped or influenced with her passion and commitment. This book is but one example of all that she has done to "walk her talk." We are deeply grateful.

Jane Burch, Executive Director

New Beginnings for Women & Children

Tucson, AZ

May 2009

New Beginnings for Women & Children helps homeless women

with children become self-sufficient, stable families.

Prologue

Would you predict that a child growing up in a severely abusive home and not receiving a high school diploma could one day become a senior vice president for the second-largest bank in the United States? Well, I'm here to tell you it's possible and it happened. This is my story, and I hope that by sharing it with you, I can challenge you to achieve beyond what you may believe is possible in your own life. At the same time, I hope to lift your spirits and even make you laugh.

To start this story, I must take you back to the beginning and let you come with me on a journey from the deepest valleys to the highest peaks. I'll have you meet some of the people and share in some of the experiences that helped me to become the woman I am today. I'm often asked, "How can you be so normal?"

You'll see how this abused child went on to accomplish incredible goals, meet influential people, and make the best of a broken family. Ironically, this is a family that still functions today, in spite of the early years.

Regardless of your own history, I hope this book will motivate you, provide insight, or reinforce the path you're on today. Whatever your age, or your position on your career path, we're all the same in one way. We have the power to make a difference in the world, either in someone else's life or our own. There might be someone worth pursuing who can help you make a change, or you can make a different choice that can affect the rest of your life.

For each of us, life is full of choices. We decide what we want to do. We decide who we want in our lives. We decide where we want to go and how we want to get there. We are the masters of our choices, and no one else. There are always people who can influence us, whether in a positive or negative way, but the ultimate choice is ours.

We must remember that every day serves as preparation for our journey, and each journey is fraught with inevitable obstacles. Our insecurities lurk in every corner. We feel anxious, sad or overwhelmed. Or we live in denial, with subtle sabotages running through our minds, trying to convince us things are not that bad, ultimately robbing us of the potential to wake up every morning with a sense of purpose and the knowledge that opportunities can exist in the day that lies ahead.

No matter where you are or who you are, I hope you appreciate this book as a labor of love and let my story inspire you to make a different choice or employ a new idea in your own life. I promise to do everything I can to make your trip worthwhile.

There are books that take their place on my bookshelves and then there are those that I keep nearby for quick reference. I hope this is a book you will keep nearby.

Ellen Kirton

Tuscon, AZ

July, 2009

"Wow, I am pretty"

Choice #1:

Being Beautiful is a Choice

I've been asked by many people over the years to tell my story so I can help others. Well, here I am at last. I was born in New York. At age 3, I had two brothers. Mickey was two years older, and Pat was my twin. Although Mickey and I looked more similar with our light Irish coloring, Pat and the other siblings born after us had dark hair and dark eyes.

When Mickey was 5, he was tragically killed in a fire. He and some friends were playing with rags and kerosene, which were used in those days to fuel the incinerators in the basement of the high-rise apartment where we lived. One boy lit a match and Mickey became a running torch. Pat and I would never be the same because of the resulting conditions at home from this tragedy.

For who knows how many reasons, my father became a Jekyll-and-Hyde alcoholic. Although he was a genius, his mood swings could be catastrophic. He had been born on the way over from Ireland. His dad died on the trip, and his mom passed away within three years. My father was raised by a maiden aunt. As a young man, he joined the U.S. Marine Corps, served in World War II, and came home injured. He met my mother and they married and settled in Astoria, N.Y., where they started a family.

The abuse started early for me. When I was 5, my father began fondling me, and this turned into rape. I felt something was odd but didn't know enough to question what was happening. This went on for some time. As the family grew, eventually to a total of seven children, with four girls and three boys, it became my mission in life to protect my sisters from my dad. This was a heavy burden for a young girl to carry, but I did so with a full heart.

I might also mention that he abused my mom, too, in horrible ways. Besides enduring mental abuse, she was frequently beaten and even cut up, and she never had a day when she didn't shrink away from the world. She therefore could do nothing to help my circumstances. My mom was truly more of a victim than I was because God gave me the strength to handle whatever came along. My mother was more vulnerable and continued to live the life of a victim for the rest of her days.

All Kinds of Prisons

After Mickey's death, my mom, my brother Pat and I were already living in fear, and we didn't dare question anything my father said or did. All the abuses seemed to blend together, and we didn't know what the day would hold.

Many years later, in my current home state of Arizona, I talked with U.S. Senator John McCain about how he had survived being a war prisoner. I'd just heard him speak at a gathering of Eagle Scouts, and I watched the young men's faces as they listened to his story about his confinement in a prison camp. He really made an impact on them.

When I spoke with him privately, I told Senator McCain my situation had been similar, although the walls of my prison had been invisible. We agreed there are all kinds of prisons, and I saw the look of true understanding and compassion in his eyes. He was really listening to me.

I asked how he had held on for so long. He said he'd stayed focused on the small things, like the next conversation with one of his fellow prisoners or looking forward to the day when he would again share a meal with his wife. I told him that was just what I had done to survive. I would look forward to any small thing. For instance, I loved school and anticipated the next book report or class discussion. These were safe environments for me.

My twin brother lived such a tormented, short life. Pat died in a car crash at just 25 years old. While we were growing up, after Mickey's death, my father said to Pat over and over, "I've lost my only son." How do you live with that? As I write this, tears stream down my face while I remember all the abuses he took. Pat used to run away from home all the time. Can you blame him? He was more like my mom, not as strong as me.

The last straw was when he was about 16. It began with my parents going out drinking, as they so often did after I got home from work. Even though I worked full time, I was not allowed to go to sleep until they got home, very often when the bar closed at 2 a.m. Then before I knew it, it was time to get up and go to work.

We really never knew what to expect when our parents got home. Being of higher-than-average intelligence, my dad could be prolific and engaging, and he could talk for hours. Or he could come home and throw you across the room, as he did to me "just because you are your mother's daughter."

On this day, my dad came home in a very black mood. His "target" that night was Pat. We never knew who his "victim" would be on any given night. There really wasn't even a reason for his anger. He had me sit in a chair on one side of the kitchen and Pat was across on the other side. He told me to sit still and not move. He beat my brother until Pat's eye bulged from its socket. My dad then went to bed and told me I could not get up and Pat just had to sit there.

I waited until I could hear him snoring and called my boyfriend, Ken. He came right over, and we did what we could for Pat and took him to the hospital. There were no laws or protections then for abuse to children, so no questions were asked about how this had happened. They fixed him up and I took him to his friend's house. I told him never to come home again. He loved us and that was difficult.

He roamed the country for the next so many years. There were good times and bad times, but when he died he had finally found peace, and for that I was glad.

I remember the day he died. I was in a church in Oklahoma and he was in Washington state, where he lived and worked. A car ran a red light and broadsided his convertible. As is common with twins, I knew the minute he died. I left the service and went to the lobby, where I sat on the steps. Shortly afterward, the call came.

Pat's body was shipped back to Massachusetts, where my parents and siblings lived. His injuries were so severe that the funeral home normally would have recommended a closed casket. However, we all wanted him to be made presentable. I, for one, had to see him to say goodbye. Pat was now free from his prison and at peace.

My mom's prison, on the other hand, was one from which she never really recovered. In order to get through the days, she would often drink vodka in her coffee. I was always so concerned for her. She was a delicate creature. She was a beautiful woman who wanted so little and could find pleasure in simple things such as feeding birds, reading, or playing bingo, all of which she did until the end.

She could not face confrontation of any type. She was like a scared rabbit. It was difficult for her to accept being touched. You've probably experienced this when you've gone to hug someone and that person has shrunk back. That was how my mom was. I wanted so much for her to be happy, and later I believe I was able to help her accomplish some of that, given her inner fears.

Early Choices

Since my dad spent so much of the money he made either drinking or gambling or a combination thereof, it caused us to be considered "poor kids" at school. Pat and I were in different classes because it was customary for schools to separate twins at the time, and yet we experienced many of the same things. One of them was that as poor kids who were given free cookies and milk and often free lunches, we had to go in a special line to get ours and hand in the slip of paper they gave us. This meant everyone in the class knew we were poor and they would call us awful names.

At the same time, what a treat the cookies were, and so we endured the taunting to enjoy every morsel. The cookies were shaped liked windmills and had almonds in them, and they came with a container of milk. I would make this snack last for minutes as I took small nibbles and relished the taste. Wow, what a conflict of emotions for a little girl and boy to have to abide.

Most of my adult life, people have said to me, "Ellen you always look so nice." How did this come about? Living in New York City in the 1950s and '60s was no picnic for a young girl. The kids could be so mean. This would include teasing us about our clothes, our name, and even when I had to wear an awful flesh colored-patch over the left side of my face to treat lazy eye.

One day, when I was about 13, I was walking to school in a skirt at least two sizes too big for me. I held it up with a big safety pin. I didn't have a second pin for my slip. As I walked along, my slip fell to the ground. Everyone around me laughed. I was so humiliated. I made up my mind that day that whatever it took, I'd never let something like that happen to me again. So I make it a personal choice always to look my best, dressed up or dressed down.

Even 40 to 50 years ago, there were gangs and rough kids in New York City. Amazingly, the female gangs were in some ways more violent and dangerous than those made up of boys. A girl in one of my classes was even convicted of murder.

Female gangs would single out someone to attack – it could be for no reason at all, or a wrong look, it didn't matter. The girl would be caught alone and beaten. Then they would strip her and she would have to find her way home. That was often more damaging than the beating itself. I saw this happen once, and wow did it scare me!

One day when I was around 12 years old, I was coming home from school and decided to take a shortcut through the park. At least half a dozen girls, some of them my classmates, congregated around the wading pool. It was warm outside and I was just minding my own business. They called me over. I was reluctant to go but afraid not to obey them.

To put this into some perspective, at that time it was the sweater era. Girls would wear sweater sets along with bras that made their breasts look fuller and pointy. In order to accomplish this, some girls would stuff their bras with tissues, handkerchiefs, whatever worked and looked as natural as possible. You may be thinking, how can pointy breasts look natural? It was just the fad of the day.

I had always been well-endowed. At that young age, I was already at least a 32C or D. Well, the girls said to me, "You'll have to stop wearing those falsies!" I didn't know quite what to say and just answered the truth: "I'm not wearing any falsies." This made them mad, so a few of them picked me up and tossed me into the wading pool.

Well, of course, no falsies floated to the surface as they expected; I was deeply humiliated because I was wearing white and it was that time of month. All of a sudden, the water in the wading pool turned red as the blood seeped through. Not only did I have to face that moment, but I had to walk the rest of the way home with a stained skirt and socks. It really shocked me that girls could be so mean. Was there anywhere safe?

Cinderella Story

One day when I was about 7 years old, I was walking home from school by myself. The street where I lived had large gravel embedded in the concrete. A boy stopped me. I only remember he was bigger than me. He said to me, "Boy, are you ugly!" Then he pushed me down, held my head to the street and ran my face back and forth across the pavement. It took off layers and layers of skin, and I had to wear bandages for weeks. This happened during winter, and it hurt like crazy when the harsh Northeastern wind hit my chafed face.

Having read what you have to this point, you realize there was no support to be had at home. As a matter of fact, my father said the attack was probably my fault.

As you can imagine, for the next several years, I truly believed I was ugly. As a preteen, I had the responsibility of making sure all the younger kids were in bed asleep before I could go outside with my friends in the evening. Many nights, that meant not going out at all. I did, however, manage to sneak away a few Wednesday evenings to the Presbyterian Church a block away for meetings with the Pioneer Girls, which were like Girl Scouts. We were Catholic, not that my folks ever attended services, and that meant we were not supposed to set foot in a church of another faith. So I was already treading on dangerous ground.

One day, a young woman named Lois, the leader of the Pioneer Girls group, came up to me and said, "Would you be in a play?" Of course, being the extrovert I am, I said I would love to but… there were two problems. One, my dad would kill me if he knew. Lois could not know how serious and real a threat this was. And two, I had no clothes to wear on stage. Because my dad gambled and drank away his earnings, we had no new clothes, just donated hand-me-downs.

Lois said, "If I get past those two things, will you?" and I said, "Yes."

I never did know what she told my dad – I didn't get involved in asking his permission because I didn't want to be guilty of lying, and I knew he'd never let me participate if I asked him – but she said I had permission to go ahead.

On the Saturday of the play, Lois came and picked me up. We went shopping and she bought me – I'll never, ever forget – new underwear. The thrill of feeling new clothes next to my skin has never changed. She also bought me a white slip, a white blouse, a black jumper, white socks and black Mary Jane shoes. Wow! Since then, I've never washed new clothes before wearing them.

Then we went to her apartment. You can't believe what a fairyland I thought I was in. We didn't have our own rooms at my house. Sometimes during my childhood, we had to sleep on lawn chairs. Here was Lois with her own four rooms. She washed my hair and then I took a bath. I loved being in the bathtub. Growing up, that was the only sanctuary I had against my dad because it was the one room in our house with a door that locked.

Then we had lunch and got dressed. Lois combed my hair and put a little makeup on my face, and lo and behold, I looked in the mirror and didn't recognize myself. I felt just like Cinderella.

That day changed my life. Participating in the play and looking like I did gave me the confidence to see I was pretty, that people could like me for myself, and that I was smart and could be anyone I wanted to be. So you see, I learned that being beautiful is a choice – and, most importantly, that the beauty from within radiates to become beauty on the outside.

Take-Aways from This Chapter:

- It is your choice what you feel, what you want to accomplish, and who you want to meet. Set one or two goals, write them down, keep track, and then reward yourself as you complete each one.

- Stick to one or two goals. If you try more than two at a time, you're less likely to succeed because life tends to get in the way. When you've accomplished those goals, start a couple new ones. This will keep you growing and thriving.

Whatever your start in life, those lessons can become a driving force. Let your past propel you into your future rather than hold you captive. Rick Warren, noted pastor and author of *The Purpose Driven Life,* said, "We are products of our past, but we don't have to be prisoners of it."

For others to find you beautiful, you must first *feel* beautiful. Ask yourself, "What do I most admire about *me*?" And smile! Build from there.

> *Remember, it's choice not chance*
> *that determines your destiny.*
> – Jean Nidetch,
> Founder of Weight Watchers

"now that door has closed,
and a new one has opened for me."

Choice #2:

Embrace Change

You may be wondering, "How did she escape?" I had protected my mother and my siblings for years, but I had my own fears – and my own dreams. As my brothers and sisters started to mature, although they were not out of the woods yet, I could look toward my own future. What a novel idea!

I started planning my departure after my father so badly beat up my twin brother. Pat had no choice but to leave right away. It seemed my brother had been preparing for this all his life. He had run away many times, sometimes for hours, sometimes for days, sometimes longer. He once found his way from New York City, where we lived, to upstate New York.

In the city, we never had a car. You took a bus, a train or a taxi. When we were as young as 6 or 7, Pat would skip school and ride the trains all day. One day, I believe we were around 8 or so, he said, "Skip school with me today and I'm going to take you on an adventure." This was his way of escaping the reality of our home life. Mine, as I mentioned, was school, where I loved to be because I felt smart and was in my realm and relatively safe.

But this one day, I gave in. We rode those trains all over the boroughs – and on one token, because back then you could get transfers. How he navigated that, I'll never know, but what a talent he had.

So when it was time for Pat to leave, I knew he would find his own way. I, on the other hand, had to find another means of escape.

A Glimpse of 'Normal'

Soon after I appeared in the play with the Pioneer Girls, my family moved to Massachusetts under the cover of darkness to get away from my father's gambling debts. We had been evicted from our home in New York by creditors and who knows what dangerous characters.

For the first time in my life, I was exposed to a "normal home" when we moved in with Uncle Bob and Aunt Toni. We stayed with my mother's brother and his family for about two months. Bob and Toni welcomed us, even though they had four kids at the time and we were six more people. Talk about the Brady Bunch!

They owned a duplex and lived on the upper level. Milk was delivered on the back porch, and we all sat down together to eat.

It was nice to have real food and balanced meals on a consistent basis.

Because my aunt and uncle could see I pitched in and took responsibility, they treated me like the adult I was forced to be. They let me join the adults in playing cards, and I remember those as good times. To this day, I enjoy cards and games because of the feelings they evoke inside me.

Ken Cook and I started dating when I was 14 and he was 17. I noticed him at my new school in Massachusetts. What a handsome guy he was, and really very nice and a great dancer. I was tickled pink when he asked me out, given that I wasn't well-dressed, did not have a welcoming family, and had such low self-esteem. My new resolve to be whoever I wanted to be, after my Cinderella experience in New York, was still too new to have taken hold.

This was a major first step for me. At last, someone thought I was very pretty and wanted me in his life. I can still see Ken in his khakis and cotton button-down shirt, which I later learned he pressed himself. Very dapper. He was pretty comfortable in his own skin, although at the same time, quite impressionable. Funny the things you remember more than 40 years later.

I also remember his car, the longest automobile I'd ever been in. It was a two-tone Oldsmobile convertible. I relished the feel of the wind blowing against my skin when we'd drive to parks or the A&W hamburger stand. Girls didn't like our teased hair blowing around in those days – after all, I spent every evening wrapping my hair in tissue paper so it would set in place the next morning.

But when I rode in Ken's convertible with the top down, I would just tie a scarf around my head and enjoy the wonderful warm day. Talk about a sense of freedom – this was the best!

In the Face of Adversity

Even in Massachusetts, I considered school a safe haven and spent as much time there as I could. I really enjoyed school on so many levels. I loved homework projects (okay, I must have been crazy!) because of the sense of completion and success. Being a straight-A student, I often frustrated my teachers in high school because I was considered a "know-it-all." I craved the attention I couldn't get at home.

I remember my English teacher saying to me, "Ellen, no one is worth a 100 percent grade." So he'd give me the requisite 99 percent instead. If the test was subjective, I could understand, but it was made up of right or wrong answers. How could I get a 99 percent if I got all the answers right? He probably couldn't know the effect his comments would have on me. I strove even harder to get his acceptance. Really, looking back, a 99 percent was an "A" just like a 100 percent grade, so it shouldn't have mattered at all.

I've enjoyed academic learning all my life, and there were plenty of outside influences who gave me a fundamental zest to grow intellectually. I always wanted to be surrounded by those who could carry on an informed conversation. Even in my days as a young mother, I preferred to talk business with the men instead of discussing babies with the women.

Unfortunately, having skipped two grades and approaching graduation at age 16, I was forced to quit school at 15 and go to work in a shoe factory. A teacher had secured a college scholarship for me and I had to decline it. There was no discussion at home. My father simply told me I'd be starting work the following week.

No school! This threw me into another type of survival mode. It was the early 1960s, and I was making just over a dollar an hour minimum wage. I was allowed to keep $1 a week out of my take-home pay. The rest was handed over to my father. Each week, I looked forward to taking that dollar and buying a carnation for my mother and a pair of stockings for myself – the stockings ran so easily then and needed to be replaced frequently.

The end result was that I did not earn a high school diploma, even with a very high IQ. This was definitely a lost opportunity. Later I would go on to take a variety of college courses to help my advancement in banking. I would not let this bitter disappointment keep me from succeeding professionally.

Gotta Get Out!

Through it all, Ken was always there for me. He proved this in a very real way when I finally decided to leave home. He and I talked about my decision and discussed it with his folks. They agreed I could move in with them.

It wasn't going to be that easy, though. Keep in mind, I was staying around to help protect my siblings. With Mickey and Pat and me gone, the rest of the children would be left to fend for themselves. When I was 17, Eileen was 12, Karen was 9, Mary J was 3 and Tom was just 1.

The final decision came after I fell down about 40 concrete stairs. The duplex where we lived was on a high hill. Instead of taking the safest way down, where a sidewalk sloped to the street, I chose a shortcut down the steps. To this day, I still don't know whether my fall was an accident or something I allowed to happen. I was still reeling from what my dad had done to Pat.

I was very banged up. When my father saw me all bruised and bleeding, he said, "Well, what stupid thing did you do now?"

Badly injured, with one knee twice its normal size and no concern on my father's part, I called Ken and he came to the house. He said we should go to the hospital. I took my hidden piggy bank with what little money I had saved, and Ken pitched in a little extra he had stowed away from his part-time job.

At the hospital, they told me to stay off the leg for three days because it was badly injured. I went home, and my father told me it had been stupid for me to go to the hospital. He gave me chores to do, including one that required me to get on a stepstool to fix the plastic curtains that hung at our kitchen windows.

I was in so much pain that this was the last straw. I decided at that moment to leave. Soon after, I called Ken and said I had to go. I put on a dress and a sweater and left. I had no stockings, coat or head covering, and it was the dead of winter in New England with a bad snowstorm coming. Ken took me to the bus station and bought me a ticket to New York.

I was headed to see Dorothy, our former neighbor from across the street. She was always easy to talk to, and she had taken me under her wing. I remember as far back as when I was 11, she treated me with respect, like I was older and responsible. Her mother stayed with her in the front room, where she was bedridden, and I'd stop and say hi to her as Dorothy and I made our way to the kitchen in the back of her house for our visits.

When I called Dorothy from Massachusetts, she said, "You're welcome to come here." Because I was dressed so poorly and the dampness and cold got to me, I contracted walking pneumonia. By the time I got to New York, I was pretty ill. Dorothy called her doctor, who did house calls in those days. He said I was very ill indeed and might not make it through the night.

Dorothy called my dad because she knew he'd be looking for me. She told him how very ill I was and he said he didn't care, to get me on a bus right away and send me home. After all, I was a breadwinner and the chief baby sitter.

Dorothy was distressed and said I wasn't going anywhere until I was better, so she called my dad back and said I was staying until the doctor said I was well enough to go. By then, my dad had reported that I'd been kidnapped, and the police had issued a 13-state alarm. I was so concerned for Dorothy. As soon as I felt I could travel, about 10 days later, I decided to get back to Massachusetts. Because of the alert, I had to disguise myself with a scarf and dark glasses. I was in terror, and that was one of the longest journeys of my life.

Ken picked me up at the bus station and took me to his parents' house, and they called the state police. After Ken's parents found out all the trouble my dad was in, and that he had escalated from gambling to bookmaking in Massachusetts, they shared all of this with the state police. Remember, this was a small town, and 40-plus years ago things were done differently. The state police went to see my father and basically threatened him that if he pursued trying to get me back, they would pursue him for gambling-related charges.

I stayed with Ken's family. His sister Sandy and I shared a room until Ken and I married in March 1966. Ken's family became mine. I could stop living in daily fear. I was still afraid of my dad, and would be for many years to come, but my new life had begun.

California, Here I Come

Ken's dad worked for ITT Cannon Electric, and Ken's parents owned their house – wow, that was a big deal to me. Ken Sr. got transferred to Southern California, so we all moved there to the land of opportunity. Ken and I got jobs with Technicolor and stayed with his folks for about six months until we could save up for a car and then an apartment. What a delight, my very own place. Those first towels … how can I describe what it feels like to buy new towels and put them up to your face and feel the softness for the first time? And to have this happen in a safe place?

I thought and worried about home and fought migraines for some time until, one by one, my siblings grew up and made their adult choices. My father finally quit drinking about three years before he died when I was about 25.

The move to California truly was the beginning of so many wonderful memories to come. Finally I could be in control of my life in a more direct way and also without living in constant fear.

For some people who've lived through abuse, this would be too dramatic a change to comprehend and handle. They would stay in their traumatized state for years and years to come. I was motivated to move along. I vowed nothing that had harmed me to that point was going to keep me from being all I could be. That was a pretty strong commitment to make to myself and to keep. I was only 18 years old.

Ken and I had been married about two years when we had our daughter, Christina. I was 20 and had undergone numerous female surgeries to repair damage from being abused at such an early age. The doctors had told me I might never be able to have children.

I was about five months pregnant when I became very ill. We didn't know the gender of the baby because this was before sonograms became available. The doctor called us in and said to me, "You have a major infection, and you have one of two choices to make. One is we don't operate and the infection will surely kill the baby. The other option is we operate and you will surely go into labor and the baby might not survive because it will be too small."

What a choice! We were in shock. We elected to have the surgery because that was the only chance for the baby to live. They operated, and indeed I did go into labor, but they gave me drugs to stop the process. That was Memorial Day. On the Fourth of July, I went into the hospital again because labor had started and it was too soon. The baby was only about 3 pounds, and babies didn't live back then when they were that small. I was there for about a week.

My August 6 due date came and went. On Labor Day, September 2, I gave birth to Chris. She was just about 9 pounds and tore me so much, it took 100 stitches to repair the tear. On the following Thanksgiving, they had to operate to fuse tissues that had been torn.

So that was my series of holiday hospital stays, and it was worth every single one. My daughter Chris was indeed a miracle baby and I cherish her to this day.

I Can Decide for Myself

It's all about choices. My sister has said to me in recent years, "Ellen, you've always been able to look two steps ahead. You've been able to look at where you are now and where you're going." Maybe that came from watching my siblings when we were little.

As far back as I can remember, I've had a series of challenges that at first glance "crashed" into my life. However, I can honestly say that for the most part, each challenge brought new opportunities.

I was once forced to go to work because of the huge amount of money we owed the hospital with four stays in one year. Ken had changed jobs and we had no insurance for the surgery, and he wasn't covered until later that year. This started me on a professional path I hadn't expected. I learned at that point how very intuitive I was in my decision-making. Oftentimes, I made choices that seemed more like informed decisions but later I realized were based on my intuition.

On this occasion, I went to work for JCPenney. When I interviewed, the managers decided that because of my experience working in the shoe factory, I was qualified to work in the shoe department. I could choose whether to work in men's, women's or children's shoes. Most people chose men's shoes because they were the most expensive. Intuitively, I chose children's shoes. The average size family at the end of the 1960s was four children. So the average sale would mean three pairs of shoes each – for school, dress and play. That's 12 pairs of shoes, and often the mom would buy a pair herself.

Within six months, as a part-time employee earning commission on sales, I was taking home more pay than anyone else in the department, including those working full time. Customers were making appointments to see me. So that need to go to work helped prepare me for the career to come.

Change had definitely begun for me, and it was the positive kind. I could make choices without any fear and with a view to the future. I definitely had transitioned from a victim phase into a survivor mode. From here forward, I vowed, I'm taking charge of my life.

Take-Aways from This Chapter:

- Make a commitment and voice it to yourself, and that will help you keep it. You may even want to write that commitment down, put it on the fridge or share it with a friend. You determine what will best ensure that you keep this new commitment to yourself.

- Be open to prospective new opportunities. It was a divorce that finally created the motivation for me to start writing this book. Instead of being moody and bitter, I poured my emotion into writing. Therefore, the effects of the divorce were greatly minimized.

- You can stay controlled and unhappy in your misery or work through it by transferring feelings of anger to constructive activity. For instance, if faced with a difficult situation or a tough decision, I often scrub my house or straighten my office. I feel better and I actually accomplish something that is a visible improvement. And guess what – it doesn't cost a penny.

- When trying to make a difficult decision, I have found this works for me: Think about what would be the worst-case scenario. Can you live with that? If so, go ahead and take the risk. If not, pass.

- You've probably heard the adage, "When in doubt, don't." Watch for the red flags.
- Trust your instincts in good situations and bad.

Change your thoughts and change your world.
— Dr. Norman Vincent Peale,
Author, professional speaker and minister

"A huge load off my back"

Choice #3:

No Guilt

This is such a critical area to talk about. Through my own experiences and from counseling others, the resounding thing I hear is "if only. ..." Guilt can be debilitating, to say the least. It is also the most difficult choice to make, to consciously change that emotion which drives one to depression and can often creep back in to spoil good days. Rick Warren, the pastor who gave the prayer at President Barack Obama's inauguration, says in his book *The Purpose Driven Life,* "Guilt-driven people are manipulated by memories."

Understanding this and knowing that guilt is so universal and that everyone has felt it in one measure or another is the first step. Second is the notion that it doesn't matter whether you actually committed some offense to legitimately cause guilt, such as exercising poor judgment that resulted in harm to yourself or others, or whether it is self-imposed. The guilt is just as real.

Guilt produces feelings of a lack of self-confidence, and this can color so many parts of your life. In my own case, fortunately, God played in my head, "Ellen, a 5-year-old girl cannot possibly do something that would cause rape." And yet so many young people I talk to feel they were responsible for their rapes or abuse. That's because they were either threatened by the abuser or they had the idea they must have done something to cause their situation. I certainly felt guilty when I fled home and left my mother and siblings to fend for themselves against my dad.

Talk about a heavy dose of guilt. My mom never got over the abuses and her inability to fight for her kids. Until the day she died, she looked over her shoulder, could not look folks right in the eye, and flinched when you would go to touch her.

The first step in overcoming guilt is to open your mind to hearing good things about yourself, who you are and who you can be. If you keep saying, "no, not me," not only will others believe you, but you will believe yourself.

I struggled with guilt for years after my teachers in high school recommended me for a college scholarship and I had to turn it down. I have since learned that making these recommendations and getting them awarded is quite a task. I didn't know that at the time, and I was so overwhelmed with my home life, it just didn't ring with me what the breadth of this action entailed. Once I was told about the scholarship, it was an embarrassment that I could not accept it. You may remember at the beginning of this book I mentioned I had to leave school six months shy of graduating. I was not completing school, and that was a prerequisite.

I felt so badly to have to decline, and guilt at the same time for all the teachers had done for me because they believed in me. While it was gratifying to know how they saw me, I couldn't get past the feeling of regret enough to let myself feel the pride I should have had in qualifying for such an honor. Interestingly enough, later in life I could refer to this with that pride, knowing I was an accomplished student even in the face of all I dealt with at home.

Replace Your Thoughts

The things you've heard about folks talking to themselves to get through adversity are so very true. I survived my childhood, physically and mentally, only because I controlled my thoughts as best I could. If I was facing something extremely harmful, rather than dwell on that all day, I would focus on something else. I have to tell you, there were days when the very smallest thing could help me transition my thoughts. I know I have mentioned this before, and you can see that taking yourself from one place in your mind to another puts you in control of your thoughts, especially those that are harmful.

If I accomplish anything with the writing of this book, I would like to influence even one reader to re-think the guilt he or she is feeling and convert it to something positive, something that can be controlled. Just as I have suggested, you can replace feelings of guilt with thoughts that take you to another place. It can be reading a favorite book, taking a walk in a peaceful place, or having lunch with a friend. As I've gotten older, I now travel, and that's my haven in my thoughts.

I'm not proposing that we mask guilt in any way. What I'm proposing is that you put guilt to its proper resting place – especially if the guilt is centered on something that happened years ago and you can't go back and change anything. Move forward.

Stop Guilt Before it Starts

As soon as I feel guilty about something I may have said or done, I immediately say to myself, "Now why did I do that?" I set out to make it right. If it involves someone else, perhaps something I said innocently but questioned myself about later, generally on my way home when I'm reflecting on the visit, I clear the air right away. It's not uncommon for me to call a friend and say, "Are you all right with what I said to you earlier during our conversation?" Most of the time, the other person thought nothing of whatever is making me feel guilty. If you find yourself in this situation, a quick conversation can prevent it from festering.

I can't tell you how many times in my life I've been called a Pollyanna. I have to respond that yes, on the face of it, it probably looks that way. But this truly is the way I am, the way I live, and the way I believe. For a long time, I questioned myself about doing good deeds all the time, thinking about others before myself, wanting to immediately fix someone's problems as soon as I heard them. Then I realized that's me. It's a good thing, and I don't have to abandon my true self because of the inability of others to understand this. It's up to me how I feel, and I don't need to feel guilt.

We can try to sabotage ourselves, dredging up old memories, or we can listen to our encouraging inner voice and then say to ourselves, "That was then, this is now, and I'm on to better things." I've earned my "redemption" by going on and doing things for myself and for others, too.

Share the Burden

One thing that hampers guilt from erasure is that its victims often keep it to themselves. The other way to face guilt once and for all – and to put guilt in its place – is to talk with others. Sharing can be a great release, and often those you are sharing the story with can relate more than you think. That's because so many times we make the situation out to be far worse than it is, or we adopt guilt that wasn't ours in the first place. It's real either way. As the years pass, we build and build upon the guilt, and it can become all-consuming.

If this doesn't apply to you, then you may have been around those who are ravaged by guilt and you've felt uncomfortable not knowing what to do for them. The best thing is to listen.

When we talk to someone we trust, that in itself gives a measure of relief. When you then hear other stories of those who felt the same way you do, or had similar experiences, it takes you out of the realm of "I'm the only one who feels this way or went through this." I found out in later years that I was not the only person I knew who had gone through sexual abuse as a child. The experience changed us in various ways; but now that we share this, we realize we were each the victim of a predator. It was not our fault or something we did.

Some just enter denial and never talk about abuse, or they live very protective lives. I guarantee you that in most cases, others have gone through whatever you have experienced. It takes the edge off the guilt to know you're not alone. It's also up to you now to move forward.

After feeling the guilt of abuse, you may transition to anger, which is an emotion one can understand. However this emotion, too, will hold you back from getting healthy mentally and physically.

It's amazing how abusers often have the ability to leave their victims feeling the guilt. A lot of time it's because they rationalize their actions and truly believe themselves vindicated of any responsibility. People who are abused sometimes feel denial of guilt for their abuser because they believe someone close to them would not do such things to them. Instead they think, "It must be me."

Once we come face to face with the emotion of guilt, then we can begin peeling apart the layers of all the things that created that guilt in the first place. For me, this process began when I moved to California. As I said earlier, I felt guilty leaving my family behind. Here I felt not only escape, but saw a whole new life before me. Being in a "normal" environment showed me what life should be. I also quickly realized about myself that I had done much for my family and it was time for me to start life without bringing all the baggage with me. This, again, was an intuitive realization, and I thank God for that. Actually I have a lot to thank God for: that I was alive, doing well and finally happy. It wasn't too long after this that Ken and I were called to the ministry and left for Bible College.

There are other feelings of guilt not as severe as having been abused and walking away feeling responsible. There are the cases where someone hurts another, whether it's on purpose or subconsciously. If you walk away from a situation and then have regrets, this can quickly turn to guilt unless you confront it, set things right and move forward.

I felt guilty at one point in my life when I was the victim of a stalking in California. For anyone who has been through a stalking, you know what a horribly debilitating experience this is. Many of you have just heard about this or read about someone who was stalked. Here is what happened to me – and although I didn't realize at the time who the stalker was, I'm telling this story from the standpoint of viewing it after the fact:

In one of my management jobs in banking, I sat in the corner office and was very visible to anyone coming into the bank. One day I received a card in the mail. It didn't have a return address on it, and there was no way to see where it had come from. My interest was piqued, and I opened the card. Inside were the words, "Your days are numbered." I dropped the card and envelope from my hand like they were hot coals. I immediately called my boss and security. Besides my own personal safety, there was the bank and its employees to consider. Because the bank was an institution governed by federal regulations, the police were also notified.

Within the week, another note came with just the numbers 666 on it. This really scared me because, for those of you who may not know, this has a religious connotation that the end of the world is near. I interpreted this as a threat that the end of my world was near.

I can't tell you how fearful I was then, or when I received the notes that followed. I was having to enter and leave the premises with a security guard. I could never go to my car alone. Those around me were afraid, too. This went on for a couple of months and then it stopped just as suddenly as it had started.

Then one day, I was thinking about an ex-employee who'd had some religious zealot tendencies, and I said "Aha." At least in my mind I could come to grips with that and hope this person had fled the area. After I informed the authorities of my suspicion, they did some research and told me this individual had indeed left the state and that I should be in no more danger.

My worries didn't end there, however. I felt guilty for all the trouble the situation had caused, the extra steps my co-workers had gone through, and the risk of danger they had felt. I did not create the risk, but I was responsible for all the safety and controls that had to be put in place at the time. It took me a long time to get over that. It helped that one day I talked to one of my peers and she assured me it wasn't my fault. She asked me how I would feel if this had happened to one of my co-workers. I told her I would be there to support that person and that I would understand how scary it was for him or her. A light bulb went off in my head and showed me I wasn't responsible for what had happened, and I was then able to forgive myself. If I hadn't talked to my peer, I would have continued to carry that guilt for who knows how long.

The worst part of guilt is that it affects so many decisions you make. During the time I felt guilty, I remember going overboard trying to make up for all the grief I felt I had put everyone through. That made others feel uncomfortable to be around me. Guilt has far-reaching effects, and the more it goes on, the less we remember the original cause. That makes it more difficult for us to resolve the guilt.

Another area where I see a lot of guilt that changes people and affects all they touch is in a failed marriage. What is interesting is that both spouses can feel guilt even when there is an evident offender. The guilt that innocent parties feel in this type of situation causes them to make severe self-judgments and maybe even lose confidence in their decision-making in any number of ways.

Since there isn't anything you can do about the past, realize that this memory can fade over the years, if you allow it to, and be a learning step for you. If, in fact, you were responsible for an action, you can take this example and grow, first vowing never to repeat the incident, then facing up to the responsibility of making it right, if you can. Then the real healing begins.

For those of you who don't suffer from this, be a sounding board for people you know who might be shouldering the burden of guilt. It's pretty easy to detect. They say little things like "if only," "I always do this," or "I once did a terrible thing." Or you see the body signals: shrugging their shoulders, avoiding eye contact. Let them know you're there to listen.

One valuable lesson I have learned, however, is that after you let them know you're there for them, you must let them come to you when they're ready to open up. Otherwise, you can't know if they really want advice or are just listening to what you say to be polite. They have to be ready to really listen and take some remedial action.

Just Forgive

There are many medical conditions today that become totally debilitating, whether mentally or physically, and this creates lots of opportunity for feelings of guilt. A very dear friend of mine's husband developed Alzheimer's. As you are probably aware, this insidious disease can take years to develop, and along the way, changes in behavior occur subtly before the full ravages hit.

This was exactly the case with my friend. It seemed like one day her husband was his usual self and then he started changing. He would become forgetful about things like doing the little jobs she left for him while she was out, or fixing something broken. This was unusual for him. Often with Alzheimer's, victims show aggressive behavior, and this didn't happen with her husband, so the warning signs were not as obvious in his case.

In time, it was discovered he had Alzheimer's, and that explained so much. His loss of memory and his swift mood swings all made sense now. So the first feeling of guilt she experienced was when she realized he couldn't help all the irritating things going on. Then she felt guilty for responding negatively when she didn't understand his behavior – such as becoming frustrated when he didn't do something he had said he would. She also regretted not being as loving as she could have been while he could still have shared their emotions.

Next he had to be placed into a home for full-time treatment and care. She felt guilty now for being healthy and doing the things in life she so enjoyed, like golf, while he was institutionalized. It really kept her in a fog and functioning only by rote. She may not have seen it at the time, but I saw how lovingly she cared for him and the soft touches, like the way she put warm socks on him and brought him the newspaper and other favorite items.

When she and I talked, I suggested she find a healthy diversion for her own mental well-being. This would give her mind a temporary release from all of the many thoughts and worries about her husband. She took the advice and started playing bridge. This would give her some respite, being with others who had a shared enjoyment.

After his passing, she faced guilt for a time for outliving him. Everywhere she looked, she could see wonderful memories of their life together. She needed this time to grieve, to feel angry for the injustice of it all, and then to go through the healing process.

I'm happy to report that at last she has found peace and now holds dear the wonderful memories of their married life together. She faced those feelings of guilt and realized that her husband would want her to be happy. He would not want her "stuck" in a world of guilt and regret. She was a great wife and caretaker, and he would have done the same for her. She also thought about how she would want happiness for him were the roles reversed.

When you make that shift, change can happen. She *chose* to move forward, to enjoy traveling and visiting friends while honoring their memory together. My friend went through many layers of guilt in her journey. Some were more obvious and others were not.

Subliminal feelings of guilt are the most difficult because we may have no foundation or basis for where they originated. A good way to approach that is to say to yourself, "That was then, and this is now."

Since so many times you can't go back and change whatever occurred, or you don't remember what occurred, this is a good strategy because you can change today and tomorrow by making your choice "no more guilt." Forgive yourself!

Take-Aways from This Chapter:

🥿 Do you have some feeling of guilt that rears its ugly head from time to time? Write it down, face it, talk to someone you trust, then determine what lesson you learned from the experience that has made you better because of it. As an example, I felt guilt for all the hard work my high school teachers had put in to get me the scholarship, only to have me turn it down. I have since learned this was something out of my control completely, so I no longer hold guilt. When you find yourself in a situation that involves recurring guilt from the past, talk about it with someone and then leave it behind with *a clear conscience*.

🥿 Be there for someone else who may be experiencing the stranglehold of guilt. It helps people burdened by guilt if you just let them know you're there and that you love them just as they are. Sometimes all we need is permission to let go of our guilt.

🥿 It's OK to forgive yourself. Others can't forgive you if you don't first forgive yourself. This works on recent situations as well as those in the past. Rectify those things you can. In the 12 Steps of Alcoholics Anonymous, there are three involving guilt:

> 8) Make a list of all persons we have harmed and become willing to make amends to them.
>
> 9) Make direct amends to such people whenever possible, except when doing so would injure them or others.
>
> 10) Continue to take personal inventory, and when we're wrong, promptly admit it.

AA is basically saying these are necessary steps for moving forward and away from addiction. These also work to move us away from those feelings of guilt.

With integrity you have nothing to fear, since you have nothing to hide.
With integrity you will do the right thing, so you will have no guilt.
With fear and guilt removed you are free to be and do your best.

– Zig Ziglar,

Author and motivational speaker

"That's enough"

Choice #4:

Enabling No More

You may be wondering why I'm including a whole chapter on enabling. I have noticed there is a lot of enabling going on. As part of an alcoholic family, I learned about this word in its most negative connotation soon after reaching adulthood. Enabling can mean taking on someone else's responsibility and thinking you're helping when you're actually keeping the person from standing on his or her own.

Enabling behaviors can be born out of our instinct for love. It's only natural to want to help someone we care about. But when it comes to certain problems, helping is like throwing a match on a pool of gas, according to Don Carter, MSW, LCSW, on his website www.internet-of-the-mind.com.

Here are some examples he gives about how you might be enabling other people, and you can see these are far-reaching and more diverse than you might think:

- Repeatedly bailing them out, such as from financial problems and other "tight spots" they get themselves into.
- Giving them "one more chance" ... then another ... and another.
- Ignoring the problem, because they get defensive when you bring it up, or hoping it will magically go away.
- Joining them in a behavior such as drinking or gambling when you know they have a problem with it.
- Joining them in blaming others for their own feelings, problems and misfortunes.
- Accepting their justifications, excuses and rationalizations – "I'm destroying myself with alcohol because I'm depressed."
- Avoiding problems, possibly by keeping the peace, believing a lack of conflict will help.
- Doing for them what they should be able to do for themselves.
- Softening or removing the natural consequences of the problem behavior.
- Trying to "fix" them or their problem.
- Repeatedly coming to the "rescue."
- Trying to control them or their problem.

I transitioned from one form of enabling, resulting from a negative childhood and undue influences, to another one based on "love" with a desire to help solve all the world's ills, especially those of the people I came across in my life. As we proceed, you will see that even when you're mentoring someone either personally or professionally, it should be to propel the mentee forward or else that person will stay in the same place.

Conversely, you don't want to be guilty of not moving forward yourself because you have found a comfort zone. If you keep doing the same things you're doing, you'll continue to get the same results.

Enabling may also be associated, as is co-dependency, with alcoholism and other substance abuses. Al-Anon, the sister organization to Alcoholics Anonymous, shows families how they enable substance abusers by covering for them and even staying with them instead of clearing the way for them to take responsibility for their actions.

I have found this can happen on every level of your life once you've been in that mode of behavior. Enabling can be overt or subtle. When it's overt, it is easier to recognize and respond to or change. When it's subtle, we generally don't see there is an issue until it's pointed out to us or there is an obviously disastrous result. You may be thinking you're just being a "nice guy/girl." I also call this being selectively blind in that none are so blind as those who will not see. Enabling is often a subconscious decision, not a deliberate one.

Enabling can happen in your personal life when you "help" family or friends to stay in an unacceptable place in your relationship with them, or treat you in not-so-nice ways on a consistent basis. It can occur professionally when you inadvertently keep someone from moving forward or allow that person to negatively influence or even harm others.

It happens in volunteer organizations when you work with people who are not team players and want to do everything themselves, leaving other volunteers feeling inadequate and unsatisfied. While working on a project for a good cause, if someone exhibits this type of behavior, what often occurs is that the work does not get finished or all possible scenarios are not explored because everything is done from one person's frame of reference. If the rest of the volunteers don't speak up, thinking they will hurt this person's feelings – when, in fact, he or she is infecting many – then the behavior will continue and the project can be affected.

In a professional environment, I share advice with my business clients all the time about making sure they are addressing the "bad apples" in the group. For instance, take the employee who is always late. There are a couple of problems with this. The person is not being respectful to the company, the boss or co-workers. Productivity can be affected because others notice this and think there is favoritism, and that eventually brings down the workplace's morale. Experts say you lose your most valuable employees because they're not happy at work. So not facing this type of enabling problem can have quite an impact on your company and your employees. In the end, enabling can have a negative effect on your productivity and profits.

Examine each of these scenarios – enabling in your personal life, volunteer organizations, and work – and see whether you've found yourself in one or more of them. I've experienced or observed every one. Looking back, I realize this was a byproduct of my youth and how I was forced into not only a survivor role, but one of protector. That automatically threw me into a habit of enabling.

You may never have had any of the experiences I've described along this journey, but you could still experience enabling – or being enabled by someone else. It's a lot easier for us to think in terms of others being enabled rather than we ourselves, but both can happen.

Once we realize enabling is taking place, we've almost reached the solution. If you see you have been enabling in some way or another, or you've been enabled by someone else, you can start changing your choices. Gee, you may even learn how to start saying "no."

Accepting Others' Responsibilities as Your Own

If I look at how I was enabled when I was younger, and how that affected me through the first part of my life, it was that I was treated as an adult even when I was yet a youngster. I found it difficult at times to stop being such a serious person and treat life with more abandon. I eventually got there, although being so serious did help me advance in my career. But I know I missed being a child and having the fun that so many of my friends talk about when they recount their early years.

To this day, I love having an occasional Ty Beanie Baby, those adorable small plush animals. I especially love giraffes and have a number of them in different forms and they make me smile. Only as I have gotten older have I truly found the child within. Even writing this book helps me in that regard as I journey back and see not only what I may have missed, but also what kept me going to what would be all the great pleasures and successes in my life. I'm truly fortunate and have so many to thank for this.

I say all this to tell you that as a child, I really lived in a codependent world. One of the first books I read as a young adult was *Codependent No More: How to Stop Controlling Others and Start Caring for Yourself* by Melody Beattie. She was married to an alcoholic and was knee-deep in codependency, maintaining a destructive relationship out of an unhealthy desire to feel needed. She not only found her way out of that, but what she learned has helped her throughout her life, and now she is helping others. That's my dream, too, with this book.

I took on the role of my mother because she was unable to fulfill this function. She could not abide my father's abuse, any confrontation, or raising us children. It was all she could do to just live and breathe every day, and she did that in fear. So I became the mother figure and adopted all the myriad responsibilities that go along with that. As you now know, one day I said, "Enough!" The enabling and co-dependence were finally over. It would be some years before I could learn to say no or not feel responsible for everyone's problems. I don't shuck responsibility today — far from it — but I take on healthier levels of responsibility and control my situation by making good choices.

Enabling to Keep the Peace

It's common to see one member of a family or group always putting others down, and often in front of people. Does this describe someone you know? Everyone makes excuses for this person, saying he or she had a rough time at some point in life, or some other rationalization. Enabling happens when the other people in the group allow the continued bad behavior by overlooking this person's offensive ways.

Women especially have a notion that we can change this person. We seem to forget change happens only if the person self-selects it. You can help more by letting the person know it is not all right to act that way. Many times, these folks keep getting away with this because others are intimidated by them. Interestingly enough, a lot of these same individuals actually respect you when you stand up to them.

If this doesn't work, just cease being around them so much. Contrary to what you've heard, that you can choose your friends but not your family, you can opt out of a relationship with a family member if it's a destructive or negative one.

At home, my mother, my siblings and I were basically forced into enabling my father's abusive ways because there were no protections out there for us. My father could basically get away with everything he did, and all we could do was cower, obey and adjust our attitudes every day in anticipation of whatever his moods would bring. The only true way to handle this was to find our own forms of escape. It might be at school where we could find some normalcy – although, as is typical with abused kids, we held our thoughts and feelings rather close to the vest because we carried shame with us. We were often hiding the scars from the whippings we would receive at our dad's hand. My father knew how to beat us with his belt buckle where it wouldn't show, like our back or the back of our legs. We would have welts that were half an inch thick.

So we did not enable by choice in that situation, but out of survival. I did, however, get out, and those thoughts of how I would eventually escape kept me going day after day after day.

Enabling certainly had a negative tone in this situation, where we had no choice but to find other options. What we could do, however – the bright side, if you will – was develop our own good times. For me, it was latching onto something, anything, that was good to look forward to. It could be as simple as a school outing. When I was afraid, I would bury myself in thinking about this one bright spot. My intuition showed me how to survive and come through all of that with a positive slant on life. In a sense, we kids invented a language of our own where we could send signals to each other to "watch out, he's in a bad mood" or "just hang in there and it will be okay."

Another aspect of enabling can be when you're the victim of a third party who is enabling others to harm you. Here is an example: A friend of mine called me one day and asked if I would speak with a friend of hers who was going through a very difficult time. Knowing my story and that I could connect with this gal and understand her circumstances, I said, "Sure, have her give me a call." She called that very evening. She was going through a very abusive relationship and, like so many, thought her husband could change some disturbing abusive habits.

Well, it had escalated to a point where her life and that of her daughter were now at risk. Her husband was now threatening her life with a gun that was in the house. The unfortunate thing was that her husband was such the consummate charmer, he had her family convinced that he was this "good guy" and she should feel fortunate to have him. She told me it was like that for most of her life, that they gave her no support and did not take her at her word. So in this case, members of her family were the ones enabling this abusive behavior.

What she really needed from me was "permission" to leave and start a new life. I recommended that she leave as quickly as possible, get a new start, and allow herself and her daughter to be able to live without fear. I'm happy to report that she did move out. She got a new job and is living in a rural community where her daughter is in school and they are both happy. I get the most upbeat e-mails from her that put a spring in my step every single time. All she had to do was to make the right choice for herself and her daughter, and have support to back her, and she was on her way.

If negative enabling continues in your life, this can lead to a slippery slope and a lifetime of enabling unless you stop it.

Remember, this book is all about choices, *your choices*. Others can influence you, situations can influence you, but *you* control your choices. You may be able to control only some elements in your life, so focus on those.

Keeping Someone from Moving Forward

As a minister's wife, I dealt with the issues of the women in the church. One woman had recently been separated when her husband left her for a younger woman. She was rearing three children alone with limited financial support. She was overweight, not working, and lost in herself. It took awhile, and it almost came between my own husband and me, as I kept listening to her "woe is me" complaints and letting her stay in that frame of mind.

One day, it hit me a like a bolt of lightning. I needed to challenge her. I told her:

1) She could not call me anymore unless she had something positive to say; 2) She needed to get out walking and doing whatever she needed to do to lose some of the weight she had put on so she could be proud of herself again, because she had told me she didn't want anyone to see her; and 3) Get a job, even if it had to be part time when the kids were in school, because she would then have her own money, a feeling of satisfaction, and a chance to be around a peer group. Also, I told her to think about taking a class at the community college in something she loved.

After just three months, she had lost a good deal of the weight, and you could once again see the attractive girl she was. She had gotten a job and started a class, and she had begun helping others in the church. You could see a full cycle occur. Had she known deep down that she could and should do these things? Yes. But I and others had been helping to keep her in a "comfort zone" that was was actually holding her back. She ultimately had to make the decision and could when she had the right incentive and support she needed.

What I loved most was the notion that you can run through your own crisis, and when you have conquered it – alone or with help – you then start helping others with the same type of problem. You then reinforce your own success over and over ... and before you know it, you realize that perhaps this happened in the first place so you could be a vehicle to help others. At the same time, it loses dominance in your own life.

The parallel here between this woman and me was that she was mired in the shackles of self-pity and it held her back. Once she broke out of those shackles, she was free to move forward. Until I stopped enabling and demonstrably challenged her, she did not even recognize she had a choice.

In my situation growing up, my shackles were not of my own making, but my dad's. The steps that led to real change for me were when Lois, the Pioneer Girls leader, showed me I *was* pretty and encouraged me to reach for my potential. It was then that I was able to start thinking about when I would leave home and make a new life. Both were difficult steps because both involved great risk. But once I was free of my shackles, I could still be there for my siblings by showing them what life could be if they recognized the choices in their own lives.

Here's another example that's closer to home for me: My daughter, Christina, is both bright and talented. She has single-handedly raised Zoie, my granddaughter. She had enjoyed good jobs and worked diligently at those. I had moved to Arizona from California in 1994. She stayed behind and went to college. Then one day she called and told me she was contemplating moving to Arizona. Shortly thereafter, she did. She stayed with me, and after about a month of she and my granddaughter "enjoying" my home, I had to tell her, "You need to get to Phoenix/Scottsdale and find a job, and you have two weeks to do so." I got her a hotel and child care for Zoie, who was out of school for the summer, and off she went to find a job. Once given a deadline, she did just what she needed to do: She got a job and an apartment, enrolled Zoie in school, and started a new chapter of her life. She now lives in Tucson and owns her own home.

Managing Expectations vs. Enabling False Expectations

You make choices about expectations. If we don't manage the expectations of others, we are at risk to be at odds with those people. I have found so often in life, whether personally or professionally, that "you don't know what you don't know." It constantly amazes me how so many folks make decisions in a vacuum. This occurs mainly because we operate from what "we" know. Remember I spoke of Dr. Stephen Covey's 7 *Habits of Highly Effective People*, especially his principle "Seek first to understand." It makes me think of the times when we all are having conversations, interviewing potential employees, coaching a friend or family member, and we tend to halfway listen. We hear a little, shut off, and immediately put the other person in our place and come back with a response based on where *we* are. Our expectations in this situation are not based on reality because we haven't heard the whole story.

I'm a big offender here, but being aware has helped me a lot. In one of my feedback sessions with my employees a number of years ago, they told me that sometimes they just wanted to come into my office and talk to me without looking for a response. That took me by surprise. But they were right. I asked them, going forward, to come in and say, "Can I run something by you?" and this would be our signal that it was a listen-only discussion on my end.

I'm such a problem solver that I want to put that skill to use in every situation, sometimes even when there is no real problem to solve. However, if we really listen to our audience, be it friend, family member, peer, or someone else, we can truly gauge what the real need is and respond to that only. That way everyone's expectations are managed.

Enabling Your Own Frustrations

A friend came to me and said, "I'm thinking about moving." Of course, my first thought was that I didn't want her to go. As I continued listening, it became evident she was having trouble with someone that she could not resolve, and moving seemed like the easiest solution.

After some candid discussions between us, she came to see that she was indeed running away and that this same thing could easily happen again. She needed to resolve the issue within herself first. She was allowing this individual to continue to be a negative influence in her life. She finally saw it was okay to decide not to continue this relationship with this person anymore.

I was talking with a business associate about the fact that it is okay to fire one of your clients. We're so busy finding new clients that we don't often look at the ones we have and determine whether, in fact, they are truly beneficial for us if they take up a huge amount of our time that keeps us from finding new business. We call these clients "high maintenance."

Well, it is also a reality that we can "fire" a friend. It comes back to choices. We choose who we have as friends.

Sometimes you find yourself in an enabling situation with a friend. No matter how close you and your friend are, it's sometimes better to fire that person to get out of an unhealthy relationship. Opting out is a final resort, of course – a last step in what may have already been a process that included trying to talk to your friend and getting nowhere in resolving an issue, seeing the friend less often, or just dealing with constant frustration. But knowing you can opt out will give you a better position from which to make a decision.

I was comparing notes one day with a friend of mine – let's call her Mindy – about our experiences with best friends. I said that although my best friend Audrey and I had some lost years because of my many moves, when we re-connected in Arizona, it was as if we had spoken just the day before. Those special relationships where you would literally lie down on the railroad tracks to save your friend happen rarely but are cherished.

Mindy had exactly the opposite experience with a friend from her childhood – let's call her Ann – who had been with Mindy through their school years to adulthood, through college and as married couples. Ann moved to another state. They continued their long-distance friendship with e-mails and occasional visits.

At one point, Mindy went through a divorce and decided to move to the town where Ann was living because she had a great career opportunity there. In the intervening years, Ann had remarried. When Mindy moved to her town and got settled, Mindy expected the friendship to pick right back up where they had left it. That did not happen. Ann's new husband didn't take to the idea that he would have to share so much of his wife's time with her girlfriend, and the women's visits grew more difficult until they became an issue in Ann's marriage. Ann felt torn but ultimately was forced to choose, and she opted to spend more time with her husband.

Mindy didn't know what to do. I told her that by trying to keep the old friendship going, she was getting frustrated and was not going to effect change. I recommended that she now make her old pal a "Christmas card friend." She could keep in touch annually with a newsy holiday greeting, which would keep the door open, but end the strife that had developed. This was really a "Don't call me, I'll call you" scenario, but sometimes it's warranted and waiting will not improve the situation.

She didn't know how to tell Ann this, so I suggested she tell her she needed some time to herself to work out a number of things going on in her life. I advised Mindy to make sure to have it be about her, rather than Ann, so there would be no guilt feelings anywhere. The final outcome was quite a good one. Her friend listened and actually seemed relieved at the resolution.

In this instance, the women were involved in sort of a triangle of enabling. Ann was enabling Mindy to continue trying to recapture a long-ago friendship, but in fact all it did was keep her in a miserable place trying to get back to those earlier days. Ann was also enabling her husband, whose control of their relationship did not leave room for closeness with anyone else. Mindy was enabling Ann to let her husband make her feel uncomfortable and awkward in the friendship.

With a break in the friendship, Mindy was freed up to make new friends in consideration of where she was in her personal development and she even met a very nice fellow. While it was sad to end an era in her life, Mindy was able to start a new chapter that was rich and rewarding. Hopefully one day she and Ann can catch back up; but if not, she is no longer dependent on that friendship.

People do change. Someone you were once very close with may no longer be a positive influence in your life and, in fact, might have become the exact opposite. It's okay to change your relationship and perhaps make it a "Christmas card only" one, like Mindy did with Ann. You can slowly withdraw or pull away altogether. This depends largely on the strength of the other individual's personality. If that person is likely to let you slowly disengage, then do so. But if he or she wants to stay in control, tell that person your life has changed, you're making new plans for the future, and you need time by yourself to do that. Time will take care of the rest, in most cases.

Influencing Instead of Enabling

How do we stop enabling and start influencing for positive results? When you stop enabling even one small situation, you become more aware. Sometimes I get calls asking me to assist someone, and the requests generally come from a third party on behalf of the person in trouble. The caller asks me if I will call the person. I have learned to say, "No, but it is okay for that person to call me." I've learned that if someone calls me, that person is really ready to listen and make different choices. If I call the person who needs help, he or she might not be ready, and then it's a waste of everyone's time. This was a difficult adjustment for me because, as I've said, I always want to fix everything. I'm learning I can't, even though I want to. So I've adopted influencing others versus enabling.

We influence others in many ways, so we often don't even realize we've done it. It was midday and I was at a retail store. The young woman waiting on me seemed a little lost. I asked her whether she was working at this shop while she attended school. She said no, she didn't know what she wanted to do with her future. Knowing that we have a huge shortage of medical personnel in Tucson, I asked her whether she'd considered the medical field. She said she'd worked a short time in a medical office as a receptionist, but that her career there wasn't going anywhere.

I suggested she think about what she enjoyed. Was it, people, animals, art? What was her passion? She could match that up with something she could train in and make a career. I told her about a few people I knew who had done exactly that and how they had transitioned into doing what they love and getting paid for it. Her eyes were shining, and I could see the wheels turning as she said, "Thanks for taking the time to share that with me." She had really seemed to be in a quandary and hadn't known what to do next. It's interesting, when we think of careers, that money is not always the only or main motivator. This young person was at the beginning stages of deciding a career, and stopping to plant a seed literally took me a few minutes and was not planned, but my initial comment grabbed her interest, so I ran with it from there.

"I can't do that," you say? Each of us has done this and probably hasn't noticed it even happened because it wasn't pre-planned. It could have been a family member, a friend, a co-worker, a school mate. If you take just a moment to think, you'll remember a time when you said the right thing at the right time … and wow, did that feel good!

So the next time you find yourself in a situation where you might be enabling, consider switching your behavior to one of influencing instead.

You're not likely to stop enabling overnight. Changing behaviors is very much like stretching a rubber band. You can stretch it out, but eventually it springs back and you have to stretch it again. If, like me, you have a tendency to fall back on old behaviors, it takes reminding yourself so you don't return to the same rut. So don't be hard on yourself the first time you see yourself doing the same old thing. Habits can be broken with time and repetition.

Take-Aways from This Chapter:

- Take a few moments to look at your life and see where you might be enabling someone, or someone might be enabling you. What can you do to change your behavior?

- To stop your enabling, you're probably going to have to make a conscious effort, especially if your actions come from love and are a part of your nature. It's easier to stop enabling in a negative situation – such as when you're repeatedly bailing someone out of trouble – than it is to jar yourself and someone else loose from a comfortable situation.

- You can avoid enabling others by identifying those situations where you say to yourself, "Oh no, not them again." You're probably in a situation that you either resent or can't tolerate. Think it through. Is there something you can do to change the relationship, or should it cease? Make the choice and then do it!

- You can avoid enabling yourself by adjusting your expectations. Do you keep helping someone who really doesn't want help? I've done that with many a person and then realized it isn't where *they* are, but where *I* am. I could actually be damaging a relationship this way. Be honest with yourself. Since what you do is your choice, you can choose to change this behavior.

Don't handle a situation when you are angry. Wait for the right time to have the conversation if you want to effect change. If you let some time go by after the occurrence, you will both have a chance to get the emotions out of the way and have a more meaningful conversation.

To free us from the expectations of others,
to give us back to ourselves,
there lies the great, singular power of self-respect.
– Joan Didion,
American journalist, essayist and novelist

"Welcome"

Choice #5:

Outside Influences Can Be Good

All my life, I've focused on being "in control" and have found this to be a valuable tool. Taken to an extreme, control can ruin relationships and debilitate you. But used correctly, control can guide you through difficult times.

Having said that, I know it's just as important to allow others into your life who can positively influence you and your decision-making. A friend of mine once told her daughter, "Learn from those you admire." What great advice. Looking back, I realize that has been a motto of mine throughout my life, both personally and professionally. I have effectively sought out individuals who had something I could learn, and they've helped me grow to be more successful in each area.

Lifelong Friends

Best friends can be a remarkable influence in your life. If you get to maintain lifelong friendships, it's frosting on the cake.

My best friend in life is Audrey Watson. Audrey and I met shortly after I moved to California with Ken and his family. We attended the same Baptist church. Six or seven couples who hung out together ultimately decided to move on to Baptist Bible College in Springfield, Missouri. Many of us stay in touch yet today.

As friends, Audrey and I could not be more different. Audrey is such a wonderful, colorful person. She's eclectic, funny, spontaneous and ethereal. She prefers casual dress for any occasion. With her personality, she could easily have become an artist, but instead she works as a psychiatric tech nurse in an institutional environment with psychiatric patients, where she thrives on the challenges of their complex natures and the core of their problems. I, on the other hand, blossomed as a banker. I'm serious, organized, and more likely to laugh at a joke than tell one. I'm traditional in both home décor and dress. I am a chameleon who can go from jeans to black tie depending on the occasion and love doing so.

Audrey and I do, however, share many traits. We're fiercely loyal, fundamentally responsible, and protective of our families. And when she visits, we love a glass of wine while we listen to the water fountain out on my patio.

Our bond was expressly formed when we were in Bible school. We each lived in one-bedroom apartments. Audrey and her husband, Bill, lived alone, and Ken and I had our daughter, who slept in the walk-in closet I'd fixed up as a nursery.

Audrey and I were on the same floor but on opposite sides of the school dorm for married couples. Neither of us had a telephone, and the laundry room with the public phone was on the second floor. We developed a communication plan where we each had a signal for "quiet time," usually a closed drape in the front room.

We both loved fixing up our places, which had cinderblock walls. You could readily see the differences in our style. Audrey's would be kind of funky and fun with colorful fabrics and homemade crafts. My apartment was more traditional, but warm. Interesting, as I look back, how visible our differences were, but this only gave us more to talk about and laugh about as we dealt with all that life was to bring. Because money was at a premium, we two couples would play silly games like hide-and-seek and squirt guns. Back then, we didn't have to rely on video games to stay amused.

Audrey used to babysit Chris when I went to work at JCPenney. She did get pregnant, but sadly lost baby June just a few days later due to a respiratory problem. It was truly a difficult time for Audrey and Bill, and we all grew up quickly from that experience. From there, our relationship strengthened as we drew closer through tragedy. Audrey did later go on to have Faith Ellen, and I am so honored to have her as a namesake.

I was glad to be there for Audrey when she became a new mom, and she was there for me a short time later when I was at death's door. She kept Chris while was I was in the hospital for weeks with a very bad infection and Ken was at school or work.

It started one morning when I was at home with Chris, who was about 1½ years old. I started having cramps. I watched my stomach begin swelling, and within two hours it was blown up like I was nine months pregnant. I crawled out the front door to get help from neighbors.

When the ambulance reached the hospital, doctors diagnosed me with a life-threatening infection. They admitted me and pumped my stomach for nine days. No food, no water.

An interesting aside: A woman in the next bed was there because she was overweight and they were controlling her daily intake of calories to help her heart. She was allowed 800 calories a day. Well, she kept fussing and fussing, and one day I finally said, "Have you seen them bring me one meal or even a glass of water?"

She said, 'No."

I said, "I think you should be very happy to get 800 calories and be getting your health back at the same time." I could always say what I think, although I have, along the way, learned *how* to say things.

She said, "You're right. I've been selfish, and until you pointed it out, I didn't realize." For the rest of her stay, she never complained again, at least that I could hear.

This hospital had a new wing, and I was staying in the old one. My room had no curtains, and the bathrooms were across the hall. It was dismal. One day, the doctor called Ken and told him, "We're going to have to operate. I want you to bring Chris down because we're afraid Ellen won't make it through surgery, and she should be able to see your daughter in case it's the last time."

I didn't want Chris to see me with all those tubes connected to me – I thought it would scare her. At the same time, I wanted to see her, and it gave me an even stronger will to live.

As you've deduced, I survived. I had a full hysterectomy, and I was only 22. One of the worst parts was that they put me in the maternity wing and I could hear all those babies, knowing I could never have another child.

A funny story, though: When they brought me back from surgery, I woke up in a new room with beautiful flowered drapes and freshly painted walls, and I could see there was a bathroom in my room. The nurse came in, and I said to her, "Did I die and go to heaven?" fully meaning it. Her laughter was so wonderful. It meant I was alive.

I've said all this to show how Audrey and I shared mutual traumas and were there for each other. There was no better outside influence than for me to learn to *trust* someone so completely. She is grassroots, and to this day she helps keep me grounded. That may sound contrary as I described our differences, but she has a real-world quality to her that's intuitive, and it's wonderful that we can safely say anything to each other, even when there are difficult conversations to be had. At the same time, I can laugh heartily with her because we're so comfortable together.

After Bible school, Ken and I moved to Oklahoma to work in a church there, and Audrey and Bill returned to California. Audrey and I kept in touch and visited each other. We're still best friends today, even though I'm in Arizona and she is in California.

I've had many great relationships over the years. Another special one was with my friend Pam Hamilton. We enjoyed good times and shared so much in common. She was a beautiful soul whose life was cut short way too early. She died from breast cancer at 54.

Pam was a gifted artist who has 11 paintings at Euro Disney, which commissioned her work. I have much of her art on the walls in my home, and it was her death that made me consider writing this book. All I could think after she died was what a wonderful legacy she had left with her art. It brightens every day for me, and for many others who are fortunate to own her paintings.

Well, I can't even draw stick figures, so that wasn't going to be my legacy. It was important to me to leave behind the part of me that loves to help others through difficult experiences, so I thought I'd try my hand at writing.

I've been blessed with so many friends who have made my life better for being a part of it. I've learned from them, laughed and cried, and grown. What more could you ask? The only way to have good friends, I believe, is to be one.

Mentors

Professionally, I've had some great mentors. As a banker for 35 years, I went from a clerical position filing checks to senior vice president. I couldn't have done it without guidance from people I respected.

Whenever it was possible, I chose my supervisors carefully. I wanted to be sure, given the traditional "glass ceiling" known at that time for preventing women from rising to the highest ranks of power in banking and other industries, that I had every opportunity to advance and not work for individuals who felt easily threatened. I always give 125 percent, and that can be intimidating to the "good old boy" network. I wanted to be encouraged to learn and grow.

In my early years, I found that if I wasn't part of the clique of the time, I might not be considered for opportunities, especially on the lending side of the bank where I would be able to work with personal and commercial loans. Women were more likely to be found in the operations side working as tellers or proof operators.

But I worked hard, putting in long hours, and eventually earned my way up the corporate ladder. I learned to work with various behavioral styles, career aspirations and professional jealousies. As I mentioned, I was born a chameleon, able to adapt in almost any situation, and this ability to work effectively with my subordinates, peers and superiors was developed through many years of specialized training and learning from those who were excellent role models for me. Because I didn't have formal higher education, especially at the levels I was climbing, I used "street smarts." I couldn't effectively use these unless I worked for individuals who were not threatened by a passionate, hardworking protégé who wanted to learn everything.

As I moved up professionally – strategically choosing which branch would be better suited for my career growth – I learned to find who was the most competent and successful in a peer position of my new job and ask that person to be my mentor. This worked especially well when I was in California and my boss watched my work as a commercial banking assistant go beyond what he was asking me to do. One day he asked, "Would you like to go into the management training program? You should be making loans, not just typing them up." I said yes, of course.

In the program, my first assignment was working for a regional vice president, Judy. She was one of the first female vice presidents in the role of commercial branch manager. There were only a handful of designated banking branches that made commercial loans to businesses as well as handling retail products and services.

She really taught me the ropes of cultivating relationships not only with subordinates and peers, but also those higher than me on the corporate ladder. I worked in the retail loan department, the area that made personal loans to individuals. Judy taught me so much about how to function in this male-dominated industry. And wow, she could keep up with the best of them. She had quite a communication style; I always said she would get along well with the saltiest seamen. You're wondering why I was working with business clients when I was assigned to the personal loan department. Well, Judy decided to take me under her wing and teach me about commercial loans. This included taking clients to lunch. Given that at the time I was a minister's wife, the "three-martini lunch" wasn't in my repertoire, and yet lots of business customers expected that. So I learned how to drink a tall glass of ginger ale since I had never had an alcoholic drink yet. I was so afraid to take that first drink and did not until I was 35 years old. I was concerned that I could possibly become chemically dependent on alcohol like my father. To this day, I love ginger ale, but now love that glass of wine, too.

I had to learn how to dress to meet business clients while on a shoestring budget. Judy said, "Buy one good suit and some blouses and then accessorize." Scarves were really big at the time. In the suit, I just disappeared. I'm not even 5-foot-2, and all you could see was my head and hands. But it was important because business owners would not take you seriously if you didn't look the part of a seasoned banker.

At one point, I was asked to be on a project that had just a handful of us building the retail loan centers for the entire bank. We took 365 branch loan departments and consolidated those into eight loan centers statewide. There was no template for this. That meant we were building out the centers, staffing them and writing the manual.

This is where I truly learned the skills of working with executive vice presidents of the bank when I was a mere assistant vice president. I was empowered to make decisions and get things done. I also had to work with the folks at the branches that were going to go through a dynamic change, and many felt threatened. There were lots of balancing acts going on.

The project was successful, and at the end I was asked to manage the largest loan center in Southern California with 90 employees. The raise I received was so large that it had to go to the board for approval. I went from a grade 67 to 91. I chuckle when I think of having to oversee so many people, I put up a "take a number" device outside my office because some days I would have employees lined up outside to talk with me. I had to sign off on all loans above a certain dollar amount, so I would have lots of discussions, especially with the underwriters.

I tapped the brain trust of many in the bank who had built production environments for the operations side. Their expertise helped me see how we could set up processes for the lending side of the entire bank. Through this, I was then able to influence others by helping them find their role in the new structure.

Later in my career, in Arizona, I found a good friend and mentor in Mike Stedron, who handled the statewide part of the operation while I handled Tucson. I learned from him about leading people instead of managing them. Since then, I say, "You lead people and manage processes."

When I met him, I already had quite a lot of experience managing teams of bankers. I was hired to manage business banking in a brand new environment, and we flourished. Mike and I spent many hours over the years we worked together coordinating the efforts within our geographic locations, each bringing our own strengths to these endeavors.

What he showed me, I believe in large part due to his minor in psychology, was how to "read" my staff members and then empower and motivate them to their highest potential. He, too, was an intuitive thinker and very observant. For me, gone was the broad-brush approach to managing people. With his people smarts and marketing skills, combined with my street smarts and process expertise, we were able to share in mutual success. We remain in touch today because of the healthy respect we built on a strong foundation.

Outside influences made all the difference in my professional life, as you can see by the way I sought out mentors I could learn from. Then I took those learnings and shared them with others. This complete circle helped me grow in many ways.

Adverse Situations

These collaborations worked almost every step along the way. There were only three individual situations in more than 35 years in banking that stand out in my mind as not being "my choice."

One occurred when I received a prolific promotion to a job that had not yet been done by anyone in the entire bank. I accepted the position from a man who was well-respected and had a reputation throughout the bank for choosing his team leaders and project managers well. I started my position and found out almost immediately that he'd been promoted again so I'd be working for someone else.

My new boss, an executive vice president, had no social graces and no practical knowledge of the job. I had become conditioned to working for superiors who had less knowledge of the jobs at hand than I did, but they usually brought other relevant skills that helped me perform my job. That was not the case here. There was absolutely nothing I could learn from him. As hard as I tried, I could not find respect for this individual.

I had three geographically diverse peers, and it didn't take long for us to see that this fellow did not want to cross-pollinate our skills and strengths as leaders and individuals. Instead, he wanted to play us against one another to weaken the bonds we had formed. Fortunately, we were a tight team of high performers. When he'd pit us against one another, we would clam up and just do our jobs. He lasted only months in the position with that strategy. Our choice was to persevere for our teams, for the bank, for our customers. That became more important than any difference in personalities.

The second situation involved a supervisor I greatly admired. I learned a lot from him. However, instead of recognizing an important element of his personality, I had to find out the difficult way. It ended up all right – as a matter of fact, I wrote a paper on the experience for a college business class and got an A. It was a valuable lesson indeed.

I had hired a woman for the bank who came with impeccable references. However, she became what I refer to as a "self-paced" individual. It took me a few months to determine how slowly she worked because she appeared to be busy all the time.

One day, I reviewed her work closely and noticed she'd started a lot of tasks but finished few of them. I asked her about it, and all she could say was that she was "working on them." I decided to be more specific with her assigned projects, tasks and timelines. The work I assigned was no different from what I expected from her peers, my other direct reports. After a month or so, she found she could not meet expectations, so she decided to resign.

I felt this was the right decision for her and for the bank. However, she wrote a note to my superior stating that she could not work for me because I was a "slave driver." Since my boss heard this specific comment from her first, without giving the benefit of doubt to the fact that this was a planned improvement strategy on my part for a non-performing employee, he called me and said, "You should be thinking about how you manage, Ellen. You give 125 percent, but you cannot possibly expect this from everyone who works for you. If they give their all, then that needs to be enough in a lot of cases."

While that had merit, and I remembered it for the rest of my career, it bothered me that he had never asked me what had happened. I did raise the issue with him, however, and after reviewing all the relevant evidence, he agreed I had indeed made a good decision to put the employee on an improvement plan.

He learned from me at that point. I learned a lesson, too. If I really wanted him to know something, I had to "be in there first." This was proved many times over during my time working with him. As I said, I learned more than I "suffered" and am thankful for the relationship we built and the growth I experienced overall.

The third example was a woman who rose to a high position by knowing how to "work the system." She would make the right friends at the right times and later discard these relationships like used rags.

We were once peers, spent some critical time together on a special project, and then ultimately became inter-departmental peers. As time went on, I was shocked to learn she ruled with not an iron fist, but a stone heart. Even with the way I grew up, I still trusted people for what they said and was disappointed when their behavior didn't match their words.

Ideally, if you work with other groups, you do so in a collaborative, win/win spirit. You'd think that would have been the case given the relationship this woman and I had already developed. Not so! She alienated people at all levels, including her peers. Her employees worked in a state of fear, which meant many turned against each other instead of working together toward common goals. She had the loyalty of only a few who wanted to look good in her eyes, and the experience changed them dramatically.

I did not have to stay in this circumstance and chose not to do so. I created my own new environment. You will find that these difficult situations which you do not yourself create help your personal growth as you learn how to effectively deal with them. Also, you begin making choices about whether to stay in these situations or find a way out. Fortunately for me, in each scenario mentioned above, there was a positive outcome. First, I realized the situation was not one I wanted to continue. Second, I determined either to stay where I was and work through it or exit as I did in the third scenario. Each example reinforced for me how people should be treated. The Golden Rule still works today: Do unto others..... Each experience you have makes you who you are.

It probably sounds too good to be true, that you can indeed make these choices. However, it's not. Will you sometimes have to go through difficult times as you navigate this professional journey? Yes. But don't get mired down in it. First determine whether you can effect change. Then do it! After that, if change does not happen, think about your alternatives.

Mentees

I had learned from my mentors and now could put that knowledge into guiding the careers of others. I'm proud to say the folks who worked for me have gone on to much success. That's what it's all about.

I've always believed you find out what each of your employees needs to be successful personally and professionally and match that with the company's needs. I would ask employees, "How do you learn, and how do you like your supervisor to work with you? What motivates you?" One might say, "I need a lot of pats on the back." Another might say, "I want to be left alone and checked on occasionally." Determine what your company wants of you as a bottom line and figure out how to get there. Get your team on board and then blow through every goal. In the process, your employees or peer group should flourish, your employees and customers should prosper, and you yourself should feel great personal satisfaction.

When I took over the business banking department in Tucson, I asked one employee to tell me two things she loved about the bank and two she was disappointed about. The two disappointments were that she had been recommended for a vice president title many times and no one ever saw it through, and the second was about her working environment. We had moved into the upper floor of an older branch. She had come from working at a brand new office with beautiful cherry furniture. Our new quarters were in a big, open loft with no privacy for thinking, writing, or making calls.

I committed to take care of both. I got her a vice president title within months, and I moved newer-model furniture from a dismantled call center into a new space for her, complete with a window. She was a special banker and these things further incented her stellar performance.

I once won a Woman of the Year award from Executive Women International in Orange County, California, vying against five other women whose careers included running Southwest Gas for all of Southern California, serving as a managing partner of a major law firm, and other impressive positions. It came down to an essay we had to write and then an impromptu interview with a panel. No preparation was allowed. One judge told me later I won because of my response to the question, "What do you consider your greatest success?" I had answered that it was the success of the many talented people who had worked for me and their achievements. Their success was my reward.

Treating employees with respect and being there as a mentor is a great gift. Being a mentor is all about how you act. Your words have value, and each must be carefully chosen with the listener in mind. But your actions are the true test of how those you mentor progress. I see mentoring as two things: one, encouraging others who are doing the right things to continue on that path; and two, guiding those who are on the wrong path or have no plans, because it's your responsibility to listen, observe, and make suggestions that can help them.

One thing I learned from working with Mike in the bank in Arizona was how to choose just the right words for the situation.

This is especially important when you're a manager. He said, "Ellen, just make sure people can leave the conversation with their integrity still intact."

I remember one time when one of my employees came in and I had to have a difficult conversation with him. He was fairly new in his position but not new to banking, and he really cared about his clients. He was still learning the ropes and, as can happen, he made a mistake that could have had serious consequences. I approached this by first telling him how well he was doing and that his progress was notable and he had a terrific attitude. My feeling as a manager was that I'd rather hire people with a good attitude and teach them skills than hire people with great skills and a bad attitude. You can't change a bad attitude. I went over the situation at hand and gave him some advice about how to avoid having that happen again. When he was leaving, he said to me, "How is it you just dressed me down and I'm walking out feeling good? How did you do that?" It made me realize that the sage advice Mike had given me was taking hold and I was practicing the principle.

We don't always realize the importance of our words. I love the story of the woman who had gossiped about someone in her congregation. It caused serious harm, and she went to her preacher for advice. He told her, "Go home, get a pillow, and go to the roof of the church. When you get there, open the pillow and let the feathers fly, and then come back to see me." She was intrigued but decided not question his advice. She did as instructed and then returned to the preacher. He said to her, "Go gather all the feathers." She said, "I can't do that; they've all been scattered in the wind." He said, "Exactly like your words to this other woman. You can never take those words back. They are gone forever. Take this as a lesson in being careful in choosing your words."

Another example of when mentoring can take different routes was when I was sent by the bank to the University of Virginia for an intensive weeklong program. Part of the program involved using the results of a report that assessed my performance as seen by my subordinates, peers and superiors. We worked in designated groups from 7 a.m. until 11 p.m. for the entire week. Your strengths and weaknesses were discussed, no holds barred, and it could be quite brutal for some. Fortunately for me, I really only had a couple areas that all who participated in the assessment thought I should work on.

That wasn't true for others in my group. Interestingly enough, the major shortfall of these very senior executives of the company was their communication style, or lack thereof. They had risen to very high levels and forgotten how to work with their staffers in a way that motivated these people and made their work environment a healthy one. One of the things we talked about was that these senior managers needed to give pats on the back once in a while so that their employees felt they were making a contribution to the success of the team.

Research has shown that salary and wages are not the top motivator for employees. They assume they're going to get paid, so this need is taken care of. It is more important for employees to feel they are needed, like to come to work, and have a good rapport with their manager. So that really was the essence of what a lot of the managers took back with them. They were frankly appalled that employees needed this level of interaction with them. They were thinking that at high levels and being paid well, the employees should be happy. Obviously, this wasn't the case.

When I returned home, I came up with a fun way to share with my peers from the program what we had learned. I had a set of notepads printed for each member of my group. I had taken the time in Virginia to find out what each one of them liked to do personally. Each pad read at the top *"From the desk of"* and then contained a picture of the manager's favorite pastime, such as golf or traveling. I encouraged each of these managers to use the notepads to send "spot recognition" to their employees. The notepads created an opportunity for them to have a more personal connection not only through the notes but also through insight into the manager's hobby.

As many as seven years later, when I would go to national conferences, some of those managers would come up to me and say, "Ellen, I can't believe the difference it made for my employees when I started leaving little notes for them. It could be as simple as 'Great job!' or 'Thanks for getting that done on time.' I guess it made me look more human to them. At any rate, thanks for thinking of that and starting me on a new positive habit."

Wow, did I feel great. This was an opportunity where indeed I learned a lot, but I was able to influence others as well. I had added mentoring to complement my role as mentee.

Personal Relationships

Ken and I were divorced after being married for 17 years. It was merely that we had grown apart. He is a wonderful man to this day, and we see each other when participating in visits with Chris, both in California where he lives and in Arizona where I am. She is our shared joy and therefore the relationship has that strong foundation. Chris has always been loved by both of us, and she knows it. Our actions prove this.

I was single for a couple of years as I was involved in the major project mentioned above. There was not much time for romance, that's for sure. I did, however, remarry a few years later to Richard, a senior executive at the bank where we worked. He helped me professionally and was great with Chris, who was a teen-ager at the time. Richard taught me the ropes of process management. He was a wizard at organization and controls. He also encouraged my developing fashion sense as I moved up the ladder and dealt with higher-level individuals in the bank. After I became the loan center manager, life changed dramatically. While I loved the challenges and rewards it brought, there were many, many difficult situations to handle. I could always count on Richard to let me bounce things off him and come to logical conclusions.

You'll probably find this funny, but given my controlling, organized and city ways, I also learned from Richard how to love the outdoors. Up to this point, I was a "mint on the pillow" kind of girl. We camped – yes, on the ground, although sometimes with cots – in Sequoia National Forest and Yosemite National Park. We would walk, climb, cook tasty meals, and relax around the fire.

He and I were both neatniks, so you won't be surprised to know the big green wooden box that held all the cooking supplies was as neat as a pin, the tent was always orderly, and our trip was well-planned. So while not entirely spontaneous, it was a new twist for me and for Chris. It worked for me because I did not have to give up all vestiges of control.

That was a turning point for me where I could see a different side of myself. It blended with the first part of my life, but was the start of new and enjoyable things to come.

Outside Influences: A Two-Way Street

As you can see, outside influences work both ways. You can learn through others in making your decisions and you can influence others in making theirs.

One thing has surprised me so often throughout my life. I meet many famous, wealthy and successful people. When I sit in their homes or offices, spending quality time, I stop and tell myself how very fortunate I am to be there, to be loved and appreciated by these incredible folks. How did that happen? And then I remember, I'm true to what I am and that has drawn all types of people to me. The old adage "What you see is what you get" can be a very good thing – or an excuse for bad behavior. With me, it's a good thing because I'm fiercely loyal and caring.

It took me a long time to get here, as you can imagine now knowing what you do about my start in life. But somewhere along the way, I had a great friend who was a psychologist, and she said, "Ellen, you're going to have to become more vulnerable. I know that is scary, but there are going to be more rewards than attacks as a result." You know what? She was right. I found that if I started talking openly about my life experiences, I could help others. And now I use that approach in my consulting business and just love being able to make a difference in my personal, professional and community life.

Another thing that has happened along the way took some understanding on my part. I really appreciate doing things for others; it is part of my very being. However, others I've met over the years have not understood that this giving was actually what it was, something I wanted to do. I was not buying love. In fact, oftentimes when I leave someone and that person expresses some sort of need, I just want to jump right in and help fill it.

For instance, I was talking with someone who was starting a home-care facility, and when I visited her there, she was still in the process of making this place for seniors "homey." I was selling my home and downsizing, which left me with extra decorating items, so I thought I would share some of things to dress up the plant shelves in the facility's kitchen. I couldn't wait to go there and put it together. We had fun working on it, and her face shone. Now how can you not want to do that again and again? All it took was my time, and now the residents can smile when they come into their warm kitchen.

Take-Aways from This Chapter

🔹 Identify one person you can influence. This person may be a co-worker, a friend or acquaintance, or someone you see often. What can you share that will provide a learning experience for this person in his or her present situation?

🥿 Identify one person who can influence you. Remember, learn from someone you admire. You know, you may think you are bothering this person, but most of us take it as a compliment when someone asks us for guidance.

🥿 Make your words count. Generally people remember the last thing they heard, so your parting words should hold value. What does your voicemail say? Can you impart some small word of wisdom to your callers? My voice mail message ends with, "Remember, you too can make a difference today."

🥿 Be a great friend. Do this by being a trustworthy confidant or a shoulder to cry on, or laugh at their jokes (funny or not) and love unconditionally. Trust your instincts in choosing your friends. You'll get the same right back.

🥿 Your actions speak louder than words, and yet words are sometimes all you get to share with someone, so use them wisely.

You don't have to be a "person of influence" to be influential.

In fact, the most influential people in my life
are probably not even aware of the things they taught me.

– Scott Adams,

Author and creator of Dilbert comic strip

"Lets stay in touch"

Choice #6:

Relationships Matter

When I had brought my life under control and was able to maintain some normalcy, I was ready to go beyond myself, and I see where I started to "reach out and touch someone." Instead of just coming in contact with others because of circumstance, I found it was time for me to be proactive in forming new relationships.

I admit it was difficult at first because I was still getting my sea legs as far as building new relationships went. Once I got going, though, there was no stopping me. I liked it.

The process of actually identifying those relationships that could benefit me was a novel idea that quickly showed results. Then I learned I could take this a step further and start putting others together, too. This new element would strengthen relationships

I was building because the additional layers of resources this provided helped me help others.

It reminds me of the analogy of the pebble thrown into the lake. The circles in the water keep growing and growing outward from the first point of contact from that one toss. Recently, a personal and professional friend of mine, Sal Cabibo, who is a vice president at a national bank, introduced me to a business connection of his, John Loeken. John is a Partner with B2B CFO. That contact has blossomed into being a significant resource for all of us professionally through our companies and the additional introductions from there. Through John, I was introduced to a prolific writer who gave me sage advice about publishing this book, and to another contact who I believe will become a good friend. All because Sal took a moment to share his contact with me.

Others help us build relationships, albeit of any type, when we are actively looking for those introductions and make it known. It's somewhat like dating. As a matter of fact, when I was at a business development conference last fall in Orlando, Florida, they asked us who we wanted to meet in a "matchmaking" session that put small and large businesses together. I hadn't heard that expression in a business environment and was intrigued. However, there is a correlation. When you're married or in any relationship, you wear this invisible look about you that says "taken." On the other hand, when you are single and not engaged in a personal relationship, you emote "available." The same holds true in business and in the community. You must send the right signals to show you are available to be given referrals, and you need to look for the signs that those you are visiting with are there, too, and respond accordingly.

You have the power to make choices about getting involved in the community and networking. This works for you personally and professionally. You will find this so rewarding as it takes on a wonderful life of its own.

Nonprofit Work

Nonprofits play a big role in my life. I have met wonderful executive directors, volunteers, community leaders and those benefiting from the nonprofits themselves.

Each organization I have served with has been a labor of love. I hand-select boards where I have a strong belief in their cause because I know I'm going to give my all and then some.

One of my earlier experiences in California was as one of the first female board members of the seventh-largest Boy Scouts Council in the country. Many would ask me, "Do you have a son?" When I answered, "No, I have a daughter," they would ask, "Then why are you involved with the Boy Scouts?" My answer was, "I was invited as a business leader in the community to join the board, and having seen the merits of this important organization, I said yes." Primarily I see the Boy Scouts as prevention. Boys who are members learn valuable life lessons that prepare them to be our country's leaders.

During my time on the board, an important influence was the executive director, Kent Gibbs. Some of his most notable traits:

He valued every individual who contributed in any way to the council, and even though he was responsible for so much of the success within the organization, he was very humble. At the same time, he had a powerful way of bringing in talent as well as the funds to operate and grow the organization.

I'm constantly amazed at my circle of friends, co-workers and professional alliances and how those relationships came to be. Just like with Kent, I learned so much as a board member that I could use later in my role with the Catalina Council of Boy Scouts in Tucson. I would use many of the techniques Kent lived and breathed.

At the same time, another one of the female board members was Ann Lanphar, a senior attorney with a prestigious law firm. We loved the elements we brought to the organization as women. Many, many of the volunteers for the boys themselves are their mothers, so the council has lots of women involved in Scouting, and rounding out the board in this way helped us address key issues from our perspective. I'm proud today to say I hold the highest civilian award in Scouting, and that is the Silver Beaver.

In one of my roles shortly before moving to Arizona, I ran the annual Scout Show that raised $400,000 and had 35,000 attendees. This was so successful because of the collaboration of the Boy Scouts staff, volunteers, the city, and the boys themselves. I had never run an event of this magnitude, but I'd worked on it the year before and had learned much to help me prepare. The reason it worked is that I learned to delegate to those who know certain portions of the program best, and I let them do their jobs. In this way, we all worked hard, felt a lot of pride, and accomplished our goals, even exceeding some.

In Tucson, where I now reside, I have a special charity that is near and dear to my heart: New Beginnings for Women & Children. If there had been such an organization when I was growing up, it may have been far different for my mom and us kids. I saw this firsthand when I met a woman who had been living in her car for two weeks with her children after leaving an abusive relationship. She heard about New Beginnings and came to the shelter. She enrolled in a 13-week program designed for homeless women and their children.

This woman had wanted to be a chef. She stayed at the shelter and got a job and then some training, and before long she had landed a job as a chef at a major resort in Tucson. Before long, she purchased her own home. The pictures of her with her children at their kitchen table were miraculous for me. I saw someone who realized what she could be, struck out to find resources, and changed her life forever. She chose to reach out and find help.

Given my personal experiences with abuse, I love contributing what I can. New Beginnings works with women and children who are homeless to help bring them back to self-sufficiency. I quickly learned that if we as an organization wanted to raise recurring funds, build community awareness, and recruit other volunteers, then we had to give unconditionally, be passionate, and bring on board others who possessed these same qualities. There were already some great board members who had worked to bring the organization to this point, but now it was time to broaden our board and go to the next level.

When I was chosen as president of the board, I began to seek out those who could help us move forward. While some were professionally successful or had important alliances to influential people, others were not wealthy or well-connected but believed in the organization and the important services it provides. I'm proud to say that many people I know have since become involved in this wonderful work.

The 13-week program helps change lives because during their stay, both the mothers and their children receive specific counseling along with other types of assistance to help them move along in their new life. But we came to realize they also needed help *after* the program. These women are often victims and do not have the means or credit standing to find a decent place to live. So we built two- and three-bedroom apartments complete with washers and driers, and we located them on a bus route so the women could truly stand on their own. Many go on to school, and all have jobs. If you think about it, problems that lead to homelessness don't happen in a short time, so it takes some time for them to find their way back and be self-confident. That's why the program works. New Beginnings for Women & Children is a hand up, not a handout.

We could see we were going to have a budget shortfall because of the changes in government funding and so had to move quickly. I recommended we hold a luncheon where we honor one woman in the community who had a remarkable story and this could be motivation for all who attended as well as the women in the program. We would also honor three clients who had realized successful and meaningful results from the shelter program. We started the process in June and held it in September. We didn't have high hopes for attendance because many people leave Arizona during the hot summer months. But we had more than 350 people in attendance and raised our entire goal.

It was during this luncheon process that a dear friend of mine got involved and continues to be a mainstay of the organization. Nikki Halle is a truly remarkable woman who's successful professionally and an avid philanthropist. Nikki was the woman honored one year for her incredible community contributions and for the way she worked so smart and so hard to become top in her profession. These accomplishments resulted in many influential relationships. She has been a key supporter on many levels and is known and loved by many, so she uses her influence to help the community in numerous ways. She taught me a lot about using influence to make a difference. I had seen giving as a business necessity — for getting your name out in the community, and even for tax purposes — and now I saw that giving could change lives. I always tell Nikki that I value her as my friend because she is beautiful inside and out. This is one of those times when I find myself saying, "Why is this friendship special?" It's because we are both real and have a genuine mutual respect for each other.

During that luncheon, I was also able to foster a budding friendship with Colleen Concannon, who owns the historic Manning House in Tucson. She hosted us for the luncheon, giving us so much that contributed to the success of the event. She even built special storage for the sound system to support the level of audio and visual presentations we needed for the event.

I learned from Colleen's selflessness. Whatever it is you do, remember it has an effect on those you touch and you can inspire them to greatness – or the opposite. This is quite a responsibility. However, it is much better to feel the reward of another's success than to be the cause of misfortune for others, just like the woman in the church who gossiped with disastrous results. Remember, your actions speak louder than words; yet, words are sometimes all you get to share with someone, so use them wisely.

Another nonprofit that touches my heart is Susan G. Komen for the Cure. The national foundation does amazing things that touch local communities and indeed the world in the research for finding a cure for breast cancer and valuable information on early detection. In the United States alone, one out of eight women will get breast cancer. In Arizona, that number is one in six. After my friend Pam, a talented artist, died of breast cancer, I was determined to do all I could to help this important cause.

I was diagnosed with breast cancer at age 35. As any woman who has been in this situation will tell you, the first thing I felt was fear. Following the common threads in my life, I hit this one head-on and refused to let it consume me. As I look back now, I realize I must have been crazy. This is serious stuff, and yet I would not let it get the best of me. I did allow myself a little time to go through the normal emotions of anger, disbelief and grief, along with some serious crying bouts. Then I pulled myself up by the bootstraps, had my surgery, and plowed forward. Work was an incredible challenge at that time, and Chris was a teenager, so there wasn't time to feel sorry for myself.

Having all that to pull me back into the world and keep my mind engaged really helped, too. Interestingly enough, I probably did some of my best work at the bank because inside I needed to be in control in some aspect of my life and that's where a lot of my focus went. The adage of turning lemons into lemonade truly worked here. I also realized I could be an example for others in this situation, too.

I know this may sound almost too altruistic, but it truly was how I felt at the time: How can I take my experience and use it to help others, just as I had learned to take my early experiences of abuse and help women in similar situations make a positive move toward self-sufficiency? When I was going through the rigors of facing and handling my cancer, I really had no support system to fall back on. As I mentioned before, had there been an agency like New Beginnings for Women & Children when I was growing up, things might have been different for my mother, and so it was with my cancer. It became important to me to work with an organization that was a critical support arm. A friend of mine in Tucson was diagnosed with Stage 4 inflammatory breast cancer, one of the fastest-growing types. She joined the local Susan G. Komen affiliate's boot camp support group and said it made all the difference in her tremendous battle to overcome this late stage of the cancer.

Healing for me has always come from first, facing the challenge; second, taking care of it; and third, having constructive diversions, which then allowed me to take what I'd learned and use that to help others. That's where the real healing begins. This healing allows you to leave the role of victim and become a survivor and, ultimately, a mentor.

This led to my involvement with the Tucson affiliate of the Susan G. Komen for the Cure organization. I'm on the executive board, and I've used my passion for this cause in my various roles. When I was approached to join the board, I was with the bank in Tucson. It was a great honor to be asked, and one of the greatest things about the position is that the entire board shows real solidarity, respect, and commitment, which makes it a pleasure to serve. It isn't often you find this to be the case.

My passion and commitment to Komen were furthered when my daughter Chris was diagnosed with cancer, also when she was turning 35. I use this story to demonstrate the importance of early detection. In fact, my having breast cancer at age 35 actually saved Chris' life. As she approached her 35th birthday, and was the mother of a 10-year-old daughter herself, I told her she needed to get a mammogram. She said, "But Mom, I'm only going on 35." I said, "That's how old I was, and you're going to go." She did finally agree.

When women go for a mammogram, the doctor generally does a pap smear first. They did this and found that Chris had a high level of dysplasia. This is often a precursor to cervical cancer in young women in this age range. By the time she went for her appointment with the doctor to eradicate these irregular cells, she had developed cervical cancer. Within six weeks from the first appointment, she had Stage 4 cervical and uterine cancer. When they performed the hysterectomy, and had a pathology report ordered, the doctor told us the cancer was less than an inch away from becoming ovarian cancer. With the aggressiveness of this particular cancer, that would have been terminal.

So every year, my daughter and granddaughter and I now go to the Race for the Cure, and we all three do the Survivor's Walk. My granddaughter, Zoie, is now a teenager herself. She asks me, "Grammy, your mom died of cancer, you had cancer and so did my mom. Sounds like this is something that I will have in my life. What can I do?" Susan G. Komen for the Cure has some really great materials, including information on checking yourself for breast cancer. I tell her to stay informed and, with the high-risk category she is in, start getting tested early.

Serving on this board has special meaning for me and I can use my financial and organizational skills to do my part and also mentor the many women I meet who are experiencing breast cancer or are at risk.

I have always been glad to leave the role of victim, transition to survivor, and then become a mentor. I love it. As a victim, you can't thrive. It didn't take long for me to see, as I was making these transitions, that people wanted to be around me more. They didn't know how to handle the victim/survivor role, especially if they'd never experienced anything like I had. Once you move on, people are drawn to you because you have become more self-confident and operate in the real world and not just on the fringes.

Networking

A big part of my success in business over the years has been my ability to network effectively, even when I didn't know that was what I was doing. I quickly learned the only way this works is if you give first – in other words, give to get. At work, you can network internally by getting individuals to build relationships with people in other departments, or externally by recommending that one client use the services of another.

You may think this is just a business term, but as I'm writing this book and looking back, I realize that I network in my personal and community life as well. Networking is a means whereby you talk with those who can help you get to a particular goal. When you ask your friends for the name of their hairdresser, auto mechanic, baby sitter or bank, you're networking. In the nonprofit world, when you match up donors and organizations – or organizations and people they can help – you're networking.

In my early days, at the shoe plant, I would look for those people who had high production and were well thought of by the supervisors. I would ask them if I could learn from then. Surprisingly, they were more than glad to do so.

Then when I had my very first job in banking, it was filing checks, putting together monthly statements and checking signature cards for potential fraud. This was a centralized environment, which was pretty revolutionary for a small New England bank.

I watched my more experienced peers and saw they had a system, so I found my own system. I quickly became a top performer because I was fast so my production was high, and yet I was careful and had a good eye and caught some fraudulent activity. I really did have to work on the accuracy because I have always done things in a speedy manner – I guess it's part of the "Type A" personality curse.

Because I had developed so quickly and my manager found out I could type 90 words a minute accurately, I was promoted to be the assistant to one of the bank's three owners. It didn't pay all that well but did wonders for my self-esteem. Again, networking with my peers helped me grasp the process quickly so I could progress at a rapid pace. I call this networking with the best of the best. What this reminds me of is golf. If I play with other golfers who are so-so like me, I golf so-so. If I golf with friends who are great golfers, it definitely improves my game.

When I ran the loan center, I quickly realized I needed to network not only with the other loan center managers, but also with the branch managers we serviced. Again, I looked for those managers who were comfortable in their own skin, didn't feel threatened by change, and were open to new ideas. They also knew how to navigate the system, and that saved me time and taught me the language of the banking centers. Speaker and author Dr. Stephen Covey says in his book *7 Habits of Highly Effective People*, "Seek first to understand, and then to be understood." Wow, I've carried that with me my entire life, although I didn't always know I was doing it.

When you're networking with someone, look at that person's needs and what motivates him or her. Generally we approach someone with what *we* need and just rush right in with our pitch.

You've heard of fools rushing in; don't be one. Instead, ask the other person open-ended questions. The answers will give you valuable insight in how to work with that person.

I think sometimes we say to ourselves: "I can't bother a busy person. She'll resent that." I have found the opposite to be true. High achievers can feel honored when you tell them how valuable they are and ask whether they would be willing to give you advice or make introductions.

While you network to attain your goals, whether it is to meet someone, learn a process or enhance your knowledge, you should always have in mind, "What can I give back?" If you don't learn as much as you can about the person you're going to meet with or talk to, you won't know how you can help him or her in return. A question I often ask a prospective source to help me accomplish this after that person has aided me is, "Who is your ideal client?" That tells the person right away that you're thinking of returning the favor. In personal networking, outside the business world, you often ask, "How can I return the favor?"

From a personal perspective, when someone asks you for the name of a doctor or hairdresser, it's important that you be sure your referral sources are credible. You've heard of the phrase "Good old boys network." This could be good or it could be bad. Here's a scenario that could very well go either way: Jim plays golf with his buddy Paul. Paul owns a landscaping company. One day, a client of Jim asks him for a referral to a landscaping company. Of course, Jim tells them to call Paul. Now this can be a good situation if Jim has used Paul's services as well as playing golf with him. On the other hand, it could be a bad situation if Paul's company has a poor reputation and Jim's client is bitterly disappointed with the service he receives. So it is really important when you're being asked for a referral that you can rely on that person implicitly because it is now your reputation at stake.

As I moved into more sales-type positions in my banking career in California, I learned to network in the business community. For instance, I mentioned I have been involved in various boards. The Boy Scouts Council was a great place to make the right contacts, and I garnered much new business as I contributed to the organization. Networking for the rest of my career became a mainstay. I joined various organizations that would benefit me in being able to meet either viable referral sources or the types of businesses I wanted to bring to the bank.

Before leaving California, I had left the bank there and become an independent mortgage broker. Because I had built solid relationships with my clients who were high-income individuals, I did really well handling their mortgage needs. I made more money in eight months than I would have at the bank in a full year. When I moved to Arizona, I had no established network and knew only one couple who were friends from when we all lived in California. Since there was no formal business banking team unit at that time, I joined the bank handling mortgage loans. My networking skills really came into play in that position as I built new relationships.

My first networking approach was through a personal reference. One of the first people I met was my hairdresser Betty, where my friend went to get her hair done. She, in turn, introduced me to one of the top 10 real estate agents in all of Tucson. I started doing business with her. And although I no longer handle mortgage loans, she and I are still best of friends. A cardinal rule for me with networking is that I have to have respect for the person I am going to be working with. Enough time and success had occurred in my life where I felt comfortable being selective about who I would do business with. They need to be sincere and credible. I knew I was those things and I did not need to settle for spending time with folks who were not.

My second networking approach was working with the commercial lending area of the bank. Just like in California, where I managed relationships with this level of business owners, I knew I could help these bankers by handling their clients' mortgage needs because I understood the business analysis as well as the mortgage analysis that it would take to get loans approved and funded.

My third approach was working with the major homebuilders in town. I set out, through networking with the real estate department bankers, to meet some of the strong builders to help their buyers. Within six months, for example, I had 11 percent of the business for one of the largest builders in town because I would go out to each of its locations every week and meet with the sales agents and their clients. I made a commitment to be there and I was. When I left the mortgage area to head up business banking, I had 52 mortgages in process.

Conversely, some of my clients would become involved in the nonprofit organizations I supported because of the way I conducted myself and the passion I showed. Networking definitely works both ways. My friends Christine and Curt Hauer are a great example of this. I worked with them on a banking transaction when they first moved to Arizona from Colorado. We became fast friends and I feel so fortunate to have them in my life in a variety of ways. They have been wonderful supporters of New Beginnings for Women & Children ever since.

Relationships as Resources

I have also found that relationships I've developed professionally have spilled over and become personal resources for me and also for my clients. In Tucson, I serve on the board of NAWBO, the National Association of Women Business Owners. The Tucson chapter is the seventh-largest in the country and is made up of hundreds of business owners. The terrific thing is that these women truly have networking figured out. They do business with each other first and foremost. I get a majority of my business from referrals, and I have a strong resource list for my clients such as CPAs, attorneys and all types of construction-related companies.

One of my favorite examples is with Denise Flynn. She and her husband own Flynn Electric. I met her at NAWBO and we really hit it off. I loved her work ethic and passion for the women of NAWBO. I was able to help them in their business, and I'm proud to say they are more profitable than ever. Since then, she tells people about me and says they need to have a conversation with me to ensure they understand their company's financial condition and are the best they can be.

On a personal basis, I bought a house and all the walls inside were white. I'm now in a phase in which I love rich, warm Tuscan hues and furnishings, so the white would not work. Since I have my real estate license, I was able to find a house quickly. I sold my house in three weeks (in these difficult days, that was great) and was going to close in just over a month. I already had a trip planned and paid for to travel out of the country. So when I returned, I had only two weeks to find a home, get all the financial aspects handled, pack up, move out and then move in. I couldn't have done it without Denise's help along with that of another client, Jan Christensen, and her husband, Mark Lamberton. They came in the weekend before I moved and had the whole house painted, switched out all the lighting, and updated the electrical connections. Amazing … all of this because we had built a strong relationship and shared high ethics. And you know I tell everyone about this. They have each since received referrals from me. There is always a way to give back.

Another NAWBO situation that has helped me evolve is my relationship with Lola Kakes, a human resources consultant and the owner of Professional Administrative Services Inc. She became one of my clients, and I was able to refer her to a number of my other clients for HR assistance. She had a dream of building an Internet-based service that would help small businesses handle their HR needs in a central environment, like "HR in a box." This also had to be affordable. She started working on the project and I got involved on a consultative basis at various stages along the way.

Last year, she asked whether I would come in and put the infrastructure together because she had progressed with the prototype and needed to move to the next step. So we hired and have a staff and have already accomplished a great deal by launching www.effortlesshr.com and an employee handbook builder. She, too, wrote a book, so we have much in common, but mostly a strong respect and like values. We complement one another in many ways.

Networking can bring about the most wonderful, unusual, interesting and often fun circumstances if you practice it consistently.

I hope you see a couple of threads here. First, I'm saying you can be anything you want to be in life. Regardless of where you started or where you are now, every day is a new beginning. Here I am at this stage of life, and I've started a new business, written a book, gotten to stage homes, and even learned how to write and publish blogs. Imagine that! Find out what you love and go for it. Then network and make it happen!

Second, build strong networks and you will progress. But remember, you must always give back in some form or shape. It may not be the same way as you receive, but that's okay. This way your referral sources will know this is a reciprocal relationship.

As mentioned earlier in this chapter, find those who do what you want to do and ask them to be your mentors. They will refer you to the right people to know. I try to be consistent in sending some form of thank you to them. Sometimes it's an electronic card and sometimes a little gift that has meaning to them so they remember it came from me. I appreciate every referral source, no matter what kind, and don't take them for granted.

So you can see that networking plays an important role. You may not be in a direct sales position in your career, but at some point, we are all selling something. If you're a hairdresser, your talent and the fact that your clients walk away loving their hairstyle are your sales tools. If you're in customer service, you're selling the fact that your company cares about its clients and you're the one to communicate that message. How you do that can change a client's perspective.

Even if we're not selling a product or service, we might be selling someone on an idea. Just think how you have to use selling skills to get your kids to eat vegetables. Comedian Jerry Seinfeld's wife, Jessica, wrote a book called *Deceptively Delicious: Simple Secrets to Get Your Kids Eating Good Food*. She was determined that her kids were going to get healthy food one way or another, so she started secretly baking healthy ingredients into favorite things like cookies. Then she had to sell the kids on the fact that they were going to love these cookies.

Take-Aways from This Chapter:

Look at one relationship you have that can be expanded. It could be personal, where you can meet other friends; professional, where you can find a mentor or fill a need; or community-based, where you can do more. For instance, if you love reading, you can talk to a volunteer coordinator about helping with literacy.

🥿 Identify one relationship where you can give back. You may be close to someone who often helps you by referring a variety of resources. Thank that person. It can be as simple as a quick note or e-mail or e-card, or a small memento. It says that you value the relationship. Complacency can occur when we take advantage of others, however innocently or unconsciously.

🥿 Answers can be right in front of you. Often we don't ask questions because we don't want others to know that we don't have the answer or that we will look inept in some way. The opposite occurs. You will make the people you are asking feel good because you trusted them and relied on their answer.

🥿 Look "available." In almost every conversation, someone will share an experience about another person you do not know. Is this someone you should know? You can show that you want to simply by asking. After a while, it becomes second nature, and you and your contacts will automatically think about potential links.

I am who my friends are. I speak their language, and I wear their clothes. I share their opinions and their habits. From this moment forward, I will choose to associate with people whose lives and lifestyles I admire. If I associate with chickens, I will learn to scratch at the ground and squabble over crumbs. If I associate with eagles, I will learn to soar to greater heights. I am an eagle. It is my destiny to fly.

Andy Andrews, author and speaker
The Traveler's Gift

"I'm following my dream"

Choice # 7:

Let Passion Be Your Guide

Passion is a strong driver. It has driven me all my life in many different ways. It is the motivating force behind success and satisfaction in jobs, happiness in your heart, and a real sense of fulfillment.

The reason superstar athletes are such profound winners is that they love what they do. Think about the Olympics. In order for contenders to even reach the Olympics, they have to have a passion for their sport. When you think about the hours and hours they practice and train for each trial along the way, it is overwhelming. If they didn't possess an abundance of passion, they could not possibly endure these regimens.

Why start the choice about passion with such an extreme example? To make the point about how passion is a great motivator. Look at physicians. They're required to put in a grueling 12 to

16 years of education, training and on-the-job internship and residency. Someone has to be passionate about wanting to work to serve others to go through this relentless discipline.

Another example is a missionary. When you consider that many missionaries leave behind the comfort of their home, often the security of their country, and the company of their family and friends to serve God and make a difference in the lives of others, passion has to be their driving force.

In our everyday lives, we, too, can live our passion. I have a couple of overriding passions. One is to truly help others. As a child, I fulfilled this passion in a crisis mode, but I can honestly say I never resented helping my mom and my siblings. Actually I was passionate about trying to safeguard them. That passion has been complemented by my need to be in control as much as possible – a characteristic that can come in handy in so many ways. It lets me be in charge of myself when "life" happens, and it lets me feel comfortable stepping in to help others in need. You've seen lots of examples of that for me.

I've found that exercising my passions has led to a richer, fuller life, and it can do the same for you if you allow it to and follow your own passions.

I've mentioned that when I'm hurt or upset, I turn these emotions into constructive energy. It's the same here. You transfer your emotions into a constructive project around a particular passion. When I was going through a divorce, I said to myself, "Wow, that door is closing. What door is opening?"

That was when I decided to write this book, which fulfills my passion for leaving a legacy. The book had been inside me for years, but this passion had been almost dormant because my career did not allow me the time to work on the book. When my friend Pam died, it brought my desire to leave a legacy back to the surface. Then I found myself divorced, and I could give myself "permission" to take the time to do it.

Perhaps you'll find yourself in some of the experiences I'm sharing. The exact passion may not be yours, but hopefully you can see yourself mirrored in some way and ignite an idea to carry out a passion of your own. For you it may be making things with your hands, creating things out of nothing, or putting people together. You have a sense of what really makes you happy and you should try and do that more than less of your time.

My passions follow the course of my life. As a young person, you could see my passion to survive, and it allowed me to overcome one adversity after another. This takes me to my first real success, and that was my career in banking. While I got there merely by looking for a job, it became a lifelong love of mine and I was very dedicated to this career, the people I worked with, and the clients I served, as well as the friends who came out of those relationships. I found that because I loved going to work and I could indeed make a difference, this was not just a job.

I know it sounds altruistic of me to love helping others, but long ago I learned about myself that this is what truly makes me happy. Mostly, in living by this standard of helping others, I hope to influence people by example.

I like the movie *Pay It Forward* with Kevin Spacey. When you do a good deed, then the recipient of that deed does one for another, and so on. Insurance company Liberty Mutual is running a series of television commercials with a similar theme. One starts with a man who picks up a doll on a city street and hands it back to the child a mom is pushing in a stroller. A woman sees this and later does her own good deed, preventing a coffee cup from falling off a man's table in a café. A man who sees this, later helps a guy who has fallen in the rain. A man who watches that later holds open the elevator for a woman who's rushing. A man in the elevator later stops a truck driver from accidentally backing into a motorcycle, and so on. This chain of events is based on one good deed.

I say all that to show you it doesn't mean you have to be an Olympian or a physician. If you follow a personal passion, the rewards will be many. It makes your extra effort or good works you do really count.

Empowering Others

As my career progressed, I was allowed the luxury of following another passion, that of empowering others to move forward. When you think about it, this is the exact opposite of enabling. I can't tell you enough how rewarding it is each year when I receive a note from one of my mentees, former banking colleague Al Ruetten. Al worked in a remote location from our banking office in Tucson. I traveled quite a bit to spend quality time with my remote bankers who worked in rural communities all around Arizona.

Let me tell you Al's story. Al is a brilliant thinker, a terrific banker, and a family man who loves fishing. I saw such potential in Al. He had quick wit and was analytical in his thinking. The one area where I could see opportunity for him to grow was in his communication skills. I encouraged him to go outside of himself and communicate differently.

An immediate area where his style came into play was in the loan center. Al would write e-mails in a concise manner. As the recipient, you'd feel like you weren't having a dialogue but just being presented facts. It's important when working with others in locations far away that your methods of communication, such as e-mail, have a conversational tone. In this case, Al's quick wit didn't come across in e-mails. Rapport-building with underwriters was important to his credibility. After he and I spoke about this, he started sending e-mails that started off with something like, "Well, it's 120 degrees here. What's it like there?" and he saw a dramatic change in his business relationships. His whole overall performance as a banker improved because he enhanced his communication style. All the talents and skills were there.

Next I suggested he delve deeper into the true knowledge base of the bank managers where he worked. Because so many of them had been with the bank a long time, he was assuming they had a greater knowledge of business than they actually did. As he began asking questions, he could quickly see the gaps there. He focused on getting these bankers up to speed and they, in turn, really started to enjoy working with their business clients because they could now speak with knowledge.

In this same vein, his relationship with his administrative assistant was a good one, and both were very good at what they did. But the two of them were not on the same page. When they started collaborating more and he allowed delegation based on trust, it changed the dynamics. They began operating as $1+1 = 3$.

I get e-mails from Al updating me on what is happening in his life today. He has done so well professionally, and he and his family are living a full life. I'm excited for him. This means more to me than my own professional goal achievement because Al's successes touched so many. Taking someone under your wing can truly change a life, or at least one segment of it.

Influenced by the Passions of Others

At New Beginnings for Women & Children, we once honored a woman who completed the program and had quite a personal passion. She came from a local Native American tribe, and when she was growing up, she saw so much need on the reservation. After her experience with New Beginnings, she went on to work for the city while attending college to get an engineering degree. She had a great passion for fixing some of the engineering problems on her home ground. You could see she had transcended from her own personal survival to being a part of the solutions for others.

You may be saying, "Ellen, these are extraordinary stories and I'm just a regular person." In so many cases, it only takes saying or doing the right thing at the right time, outside of your norm, to make a difference. Once you make this a part of your life, it will become a habit because the rewards are so great. Even if you don't see instant change, you can be assured you did effect change. I'm sure you've had the experience where you did something really nice for someone and that person didn't even acknowledge you, and you said, "Well, what's up with that?" If you're saying this, you did not give unconditionally. Your rewards are greater if you give with no thought of a return coming back to you. Then if there is a return of any sort, it will be unexpected and you'll be grateful. It's all about adjusting your expectations.

You're probably thinking my expectations are generally high since I live to a high standard. Actually, I'm quite a realist. For instance, I was quite taken when the bank I was with gave its employees a copy of the book *Raving Fans: A Revolutionary Approach to Customer Service* by Ken Blanchard and Sheldon Bowles. It talks about expectations. One of the stories in the book hit home for me since it was about a cabbie. Being from New York City, I was used to cabs as a main form of transportation.

A woman had just gotten her own cab to drive customers to and from the airport. She was way back in the line as other more seasoned drivers had front spots. So she thought to herself, "I really want this to be a great career for me." It was her passion. The first thing she did was wash her cab every night. She knew that she herself loved getting into clean cars and the passengers' expectations were so low that when they saw a clean cab, this would start to set her apart. Then she bought newspapers and asked when a passenger got in, "Do you want me to help you navigate the city or let you be? Or I have a newspaper you may like to read?" Wow, another level of expectation was reached. Then she decided to bring a thermos of coffee and offer that to her passengers. Before long, customers were asking for her by name. The lesson here is that most consumers today expect so little that even when we get *good* service, never mind *great* service, we're impressed.

I have another passion that really is a quasi-hobby, quasi-business for me: interior decorating. This showed itself early in my life. In home economics class in high school, we could choose cooking, sewing or design, and I took design. I already cooked for a large family, and did not have the means to buy what was needed for the sewing class, so design was left. I so enjoyed my project. I could design my ideal home that had nothing to do with the place where I lived.

So I took a cardboard box along with cloth remnants from the teacher, and I made a miniature home, complete with curtains for the windows I had cut out, a bedspread for the bed, and a tablecloth for the kitchen table. I made rugs for the floors, and it was darling. I was so ecstatic. I had created this myself, and it reflected me.

As the years went by, Ken and I relocated to Oklahoma to work in a church, and we moved into our first purchased house. Actually, it was the first house I had ever lived in. Some folks in the church had given us an Early American wing sofa and chair. It needed lots of TLC, so I took on the task of recovering it, having never done this before in my life. To add to this, I bought plaid

Herculon fabric. The plaid is hard to match when you're covering different parts of the sofa, and the fabric is thick and difficult to work with. I asked myself, "What were you thinking?" So without any pattern, I took the furniture apart and laid the pieces on the floor in the opposite order of the way I had taken them off. Then I cut pieces of fabric using the old ones as a pattern. I reassembled the sofa and chair with mostly stapling and some sewing. They came out great, and our living room was beautiful. I look back and say, "How in the world did I do that?" Like the intuition I mentioned earlier, some of us have natural instincts for some things, and one of mine is for decorating. From then on, I did the interior decor for all the places where we lived, and I would occasionally consult.

When I retired from banking a few years ago, I had to decide whether to be a consultant and speaker or go into interior decorating as a new profession. I looked into all the courses and finally decided to become a consultant because thinking about how much fun it was to do decorating work, I was afraid if I took this on as a new career it may cease to be enjoyable. So I dabble in it by helping friends and doing some staging for a couple of wonderful Realtors. This allows me to indulge this passion and not completely depend on it for my income.

Here in Arizona, with my former husband, I did all the decorating work from the floor up on custom homes we built. My work really has come a long way since I began. I was helping build and then live in a 6,300-square-foot home. With no formal training, just instinct, my main goal was that when the house was finished it would look warm and inviting. Perhaps you've been in or seen pictures of big homes with cathedral ceilings. Some of ours went up 19 feet. The rooms can feel so cold. I had the walls painted in a faux finish and bought a very eclectic mix of furnishings – quite a departure for me, because I've typically decorated in a more traditional fashion.

I simply said to myself, "Let yourself go and enjoy the ride." And that I did. I bought furnishings from the likes of Ethan Allan, and then would peruse the antique stores and consignment shops. How liberating that felt, having no constraints on what the house would look like when done, but intuitively blending pieces and styles. I laugh when I think about myself carrying around this cloth bag with samples of granite, flooring and fabric. Every new sample was compared with those already accumulated to ensure cohesion with the overall feel. I'm proud to say that this particular house sold the day it went on the market. I know the current owner, and she loves it because it fits her style. What a rewarding feeling for me.

Growing Through Sharing

I spoke at a National Association of Women Business Owners luncheon a few years ago about choices, the main topic of this book – although the book was but a glimmer in my eye at the time. Many of the women attending know me as I am now, very involved in the community, a consultant, and well put-together, as I've been told. After I spoke, a good number of the business women came up to me and expressed either their situations or how much they appreciated me sharing such a personal side of my life to make important points for them.

One of them was Jayne Henninger, the owner of Remedy Intelligent Staffing here in Tucson and quite a beautiful person inside and out. A real role model for many, she was so taken with my story that she shared with me how it meant a lot to see the way one can progress from the very worst foundations to a successful place in life. Also, I received a note from Sherie Broekema, a woman who has dedicated her life to her clients as a Realtor and now specifically helps the older generation and their families through a special program she designed. She wrote, "Just want to let you know how much I enjoyed your talk at the NAWBO lunch. It was the right talk at the right moment. I thought it very interesting that you never had guilt. Thank you." This kind of feedback told me I was following the right path by telling my story in a way that was meant to have a positive influence on others.

Another friend of mine, Kandy Walsh, has taught me so much about how you look beyond what you think you are "worth" and just be the person you want to be. She is a most refined lady; yet she knows how to live life to its fullest. Her passions are her family and her long career in real estate. When we first became friends, I asked myself, "Why me? She's so special, so revered. What does she see in me?" I have as much asked her that, and she says I do everything with a clear purpose and a pure heart. It doesn't get much better than that!

Encouragement like this, from people I admire and respect, has freed me up even more to live my passion of making a difference.

My e-mail says, "Remember, you too can make a difference today." You can see a ribbon running through my experiences that show how my passions have shaped my life personally and professionally.

I've made great friends over the years – many through my professional or community relationships with them. I also enjoy hearing how others follow their passions. One friend who used to work with me and is still in banking is married to a civil servant. He is soon to retire, and rather than wait and see what the world has to offer, he decided to invest in a venture of his own. He came up with the concept through an experience he'd had. He loves sports and has helped with many teams over the years. He was looking for customized caps for one of these teams and could not find them. So he talked with a woman who showed him how these could be made. He was bitten. He decided he was going to get ahead of his retirement curve, and on his own time start making specialty items with equipment he was able to purchase.

So he is already on his way to the next stage in his life – all because of a strong desire, or passion, to have something special. The opportunity came about because he couldn't find a cookie cutter answer. This can happen for you, too, if you follow your passion as you move through life to the next stage, whatever that may be.

The Passion of Family Love

My other passion is spending time with my daughter and granddaughter. They have brought me many experiences of joy.

Chris's desire to help others has been somewhat tempered in life just because she has had to learn to live within her means since she is the single source of support for Zoie. She gives in ways she can, and that often involves donating time to my charities. For many years, she and Zoie would both help at Christmas for the New Beginnings poinsettia campaign.

Now I see her involved in our local church and really blossoming. Recently, a neighbor was having difficulty getting her yard weeded. Chris said at church, "Let's go over after this and clean up that front yard." Even though this was the only day she had to herself, she gave up her time to help my neighbor. Not only that, but while we were weeding, Chris heard a hair-raising scream from up the street. I was watering, and she said, "Turn off the water, Mom!" She went running and I followed, although at a slower pace. When she got to the small park around the corner, she found a woman had fallen down the steps of the kids' slide and her elbow was turned around the wrong way. She saw me coming and asked me to call 911.

I ran back to the house as fast as I could, brought my phone and called the paramedics. When I got to the park, Chris was there holding the woman's hand. Another neighbor took the woman's granddaughter to her house because she was so frightened, although not hurt. When the police and paramedics came, Chris stayed right by her side as her son appeared and went to get his daughter and take her to care so he could go to the hospital. We took the son's information down because the woman was here visiting from out of state. We later called and found out they were able to put the elbow back in place and she was resting comfortably. Chris did not hesitate one moment to be there for her.

The son called that night and said he was so grateful. Other neighbors didn't even come out and see what was going on. It's so easy to just avoid involvement. I know in these times you have to be careful who you trust, and I salute that. There are those occasions, though, where you can get involved and be a good neighbor.

I was proud of my daughter, and I also admire the way she and Zoie share a passion for horses. I don't have any pets, mostly because I'm gone way too much and that isn't fair to the animals. However, I also teasingly say it's because Chris and Zoie have enough for all of us.

Zoie has been amazing in her quest to have her own horse. I paid for riding lessons for her because it was so important to her. I felt she should be encouraged in her passion of loving animals and her driving desire to ride horses.

A good friend of mine in Tucson, Diana Madaras, a gifted and prolific artist, told me once that girls between ages 13 and 16 should be involved with horses because it helps in those particular development years. Diana has her own philanthropic causes, and I have to say has been an integral part in some of mine. She is well-known in the community for her Art for Animals Foundation, as well as the art she donates to many charities.

My biggest "aha" from Diana's words was that Zoie's horse loves her unconditionally. Since her dad is not in her life and she is missing that paternal support and love, her horse, Danny, is a mainstay. I'm proud to say Zoie earned Danny on her own. For a full year, she worked almost every day at the stables where she rides, mucking out the stalls, walking the horses, helping with any chores. The owner of the ranch gave her this opportunity because he said he sees teenagers all the time at the ranch and all they want to do is ride, but Zoie is willing to do whatever it takes to have a horse. She has stayed committed for years now – it was not just a passing fancy. That's what I call passion.

Take-Aways from This Chapter:

- Since we have become a service-oriented society, versus industrial in nature, there are lots of opportunities for us to do something we are *passionate* about. You may find this in the form of starting a new business or working for a smaller company with more input and contribution.

- If you're protecting your current job, showing passion in how you do it can send the right signal to your supervisors so they realize you're a critical employee.

- Listen to your head and heart for that particular idea that has been floating around for so long. Is it something you can start to tangibly plan in order to make it happen? It may actually happen at a later time, but you can be building the framework now. Then instead of being work, this could become a great diversion from all the things we're hearing about right now in the world crises. Your thinking is in your control.

- Share your experiences with others. Those opportunities will present themselves, and from your sharing, you can help others with their situation. In the process, you yourself will grow. You'll also realize that there was a reason you had that experience in the first place.

Be a supportive friend when people you know are attempting a new venture as their passion. This can be an exciting and at the same time fearful period for them. Having friends like you there to support them can keep them going during both good and rough times. You will then find the same returned to you.

The kind of commitment I find among the best performers across virtually every field is a single-minded passion for what they do, an unwavering desire for excellence in the way they think and the way they work. Genuine confidence is what launches you out of bed in the morning, and through your day with a spring in your step.

> — Jim Collins,
>
> Author, motivational speaker and business consultant

"One step at a time"

Choice #8:

It's Your Turn to Be Happy

This book has been all about choices. We've talked about you deciding when you get up in the morning how you are going to feel as you go through your day. Others will try to influence your day, but it is ultimately up to you how you feel.

We've talked about seeking out positive influences and surrounding yourself with them. Negative people spread their influence quickly. If, however, you want a "can do" attitude to permeate your life, being around like-minded people will help you accomplish this.

Another choice is spending your life helping others when you can. It's one thing to recognize need around you, and another to do something about it. It doesn't mean the same measure of involvement for everyone. If you have children and their safety and happiness are important, then belonging to and participating in the PTA is a way to get involved. You're not just leaving things in the hands of the school and other volunteers.

Deciding to be involved in professional organizations or nonprofits is another choice you can make if that interests you. Not only is it rewarding to dedicate your knowledge and experience to helping others, but you can continue growing.

If you're early in your career, then you can find a mentor from whom you can learn much. If you're mid-career, you could be in both shoes at the same time, being mentored by someone and leading others by example. If you're late in your career, share the wealth of your experience with those moving up the ladder. We women are so good at nurturing, and continuing this practice in a professional environment can pay big dividends.

As I started my consulting business, it grew and grew because of the relationships I had formed through my work with professional organizations and nonprofits, and networking became my middle name. This can work in your life, too. Networking actually becomes second nature to you.

Having the freedom to make choices can be elusive at times. I once attended a meeting where the speaker said that "discipline can be freedom." Talk about an oxymoron. How can that be? Then I got it. If you have a discipline in your life, that ensures you get the important things done – taking care of family, doing a good job at work, those kinds of things. Then you can feel free about doing some things for yourself. I find that after I've done all the tasks of the day, I don't feel guilty about doing something for myself, even if it's just for a few moments. Here we go with that guilt thing again. Don't put yourself in a place to be saddled with guilt.

The Results of Life's Lessons

I have another story to tell you that demonstrates the lessons life has taught me that now allow me to be happy and secure. There is every reason to believe I should be bitter and hard, but I'm everything but. If, in your life, you have experienced difficult times, or you've gone through the fires, it is still it up to you to be in control of your situation and your approach to it. I choose to be upbeat and live as an example to those whose lives I touch.

I was spending the weekend recently with another very good friend while celebrating my birthday. Karen Gabriel was in Phoenix for the Angels spring training with her husband and her sister Judy. We were discussing my book, and I told them I was on the last chapter and had not talked about my recent ex-husband. There was no real reason other than I didn't see any place where it had relevance. Then they reminded me of how I'd handled the breakup with grace and that demonstrated how much I had grown because of my life experiences.

I met Karen about 17 years ago in Southern California through my ex-husband. He and Karen's husband, Lou, had been friends for many years, rearing their children together and sharing vacations. Karen is a woman I would call a "Miss Congeniality." She has a kind word for everyone and an easy manner. She's also a very talented interior designer. As I was developing my design skills, she was a great mentor. This is what I refer to when I say to surround yourself with those you can learn from and respect.

At any rate, Karen and Judy encouraged me to write the story surrounding the end of my marriage because of the way I handled the divorce. This really is an example of not fostering bitterness; it can only hold you back and cause you ongoing pain if you allow it to.

My ex-husband left abruptly one day with no real warning. I was getting ready for work and he said, "I'm leaving." I said, "Okay, I'll see you tonight." He said, "No, I'm leaving for good," and that was that. He had been planning and preparing for this for some time, and of course I had no preparation. This is what I did: I allowed myself one week of crying, yelling and going through all the usual emotions. Then I said to myself, "Ellen, this is what it is, so get over it," and I did.

Sound familiar? It's like when I said to myself, "I'm pretty and smart and I can make something of myself in life," and I did. Or when I said, "I'm leaving home," and I did. Remember, there are times when you have to plan these things. The timing may not be right at the moment, but you can plant the seed and move toward that decision.

It was November when my husband left, so I decided I was going to host a fabulous Christmas party for 20 or more of my girlfriends, and I threw myself into the planning and preparation. What a grand time I had. My ex-husband was not a fan of Christmas, so I let myself go whole hog. I decorated three trees, sent out invitations, shopped and cooked for weeks. My friends and I had a blast. That transitioned me right into the holidays, which I truly enjoyed that year. This was a choice I made then and there to move forward and use a diversion to help with that transition.

Again, I was not masking feelings and emotions unrealized. I had faced them and decided it was time to move forward. Life is fleeting, and every moment counts. You've heard the expression, "Live today as if there will be no tomorrow." It doesn't mean you should give up planning and being prepared, but it does mean live each moment to its fullest.

I made up my mind not to be bitter because that just would have held me back. Bitterness is just like guilt, and I wasn't going to go there. We'd had 14 very good years of marriage that we'd both contributed to, which I truly enjoyed. Since he was a custom builder, I could do the design work for the houses he created, and I loved that. Only the last year was difficult, as I look back. So why not take the best from the relationship and progress? When this took place, I immediately said to myself, "So God shut that door. What door is opening?" and here I am writing this book.

God's Place in This Book

My relationship to God has been a constant in my life, although definitely more at times than others. In my early life, God was my protector. I would pray in the quiet of a closet where I could voice my fears and ask for peace. A funny story, though: I had read, and still believe, that God is omniscient – all-seeing and all-knowing. Well, when I got dressed, I would do so in the dark of the closet because I didn't want God to see me. So I was listening to the part about all-seeing, but obviously putting my own spin on it.

Serving through the church was always fulfilling and allowed me to follow my passion of helping others in an environment that encouraged this. I was surrounded by some great men and women who led by example. There was one couple that amazed me. When the husband was a younger man, he worked in a glass shop. He told himself that one day he would own that shop and, by golly, one day he did. Then he bought land and owned thousands of grazing acres for his herd of black angus. From my perspective as an assistant pastor's wife, he and his wife were rich beyond measure. When we visited their incredible home, I was awestruck. They had walls that were made out of glass block, and fireplaces everywhere, and so many things I had never seen before.

One day she asked if I would make her some dresses. Immediately I said yes. Then when she gave me the patterns and fabric, I was distressed. I sewed mostly simple things, like dresses for my daughter and myself. I had just volunteered to sew a dress with expensive fabric and pleats. I had never made a pleat in my life. One pattern had a diamond inset. All I could do was pray these dresses would come out all right and that I would not waste fabric because we could not afford to replace any I might ruin. In the end, they came out quite nice, which really surprised me. She was delighted and so was I.

When she gave me the chance to make those dresses, in a very subtle way she was giving me the means to make some extra money. God was meeting our need through this couple and this was a valuable lesson for me. I saw how godly folks really act. It's not by what they say so much, but by what they do and how they live. This was a self-made couple. They were a great example of how hard work and living right pays dividends. This couple treated everyone in the church as equals and set an example by sharing what they had. If you came to this church for the first time and met this couple, you would never know they were the wealthiest people there. I vowed to be that kind of a Christian.

So you don't hear me "preaching." I try to live my life by a high ideal and by works versus empty words. There have been many times when I have said, "Okay, God, you shut that door. What will the next one hold?" and I trusted and he guided me.

Where Are They Now?

When I left my parents' home, I wasn't certain what would happen to my siblings. Many years have gone by, and each of us has found our way. I know my mom is smiling as she looks down on us and sees how far we've come. I thought I would take a moment and let you know where my siblings are now.

There were originally seven of us, and now we're five. I'll go in chronological order. My sister Eileen, next-oldest, still lives in Massachusetts and has been married for many years to Tony. Their two children are grown. One lives in Massachusetts and one here in Arizona. She has been with the phone company forever, and one day she will retire and enjoy her home and family. Eileen has been the one who has kept the home ties as the rest of us are scattered around the country. She visits regularly with aunts and uncles and other family members there in Massachusetts. She also keeps all of our family information current so we can stay in touch with each other.

Next is Karen who lives here in Tucson with her husband, Ron. They have been married more than 30 years and are still as much in love as ever. They lost their oldest son, and they have a daughter with her husband and kids in Pennsylvania; they have two daughters who live here in Tucson, one with her husband and the other with her husband and kids; and one son in Delaware. It was great when Karen moved to Tucson because in addition to having her and her family nearby, she could share the responsibility of caring for our mother, which she did gladly. We had some wonderful coffee klatches on Saturdays that we both remember with fondness. She has also has a special relationship with my daughter Christina, for which I'm very thankful.

Mary J lives near Chicago with her husband, Jim. They have two daughters, one in Virginia and one there living nearby who bought her first house at 21. Mary J has overcome many challenges in her life, for which I'm very proud of her.

Lastly, the youngest is my brother Tom, who lives in New Hampshire. He is divorced and has one daughter in Massachusetts. Tom wrote a wonderful play and got it produced.

I'm quite proud of all of them, especially given our start in life. Each one of us has our own story to tell, so I'm not telling theirs, but I include them in my story because they are a very important part of my life. I value each of them. There are different relationships with each, and that's because we are all in different places in our lives, so we stay close and are there for each other during important events if not in everyday life.

Baby Steps

We have covered much, and I wanted to be sure to suggest you take baby steps as you embrace this thought of choices. You don't have to do it all at once. I sincerely hope you have read some takeaways that you can employ yourself. If so, give it some thought and then take one step at a time.

I shared with you that when I am helping a young person suffering through difficult times, I ask her to first make her home a haven. This is a pretty quick thing that can be done with instant results that make you feel good. Then I say to take just one school course. The idea of going to college and a taking a full load can be daunting and impractical. But completing one course gives you an immediate feeling of satisfaction and pride, and it might spur you to enroll in a second one.

Another baby step that makes me feel good pretty quickly is cleaning out my closet. This is especially if I have lost weight and can get rid of those larger clothes – oh, how liberating. Either way, just straightening, organizing and decluttering gives me a visible sign that I have progressed.

For me, another baby step way back when I first left home was buying those new towels and putting them next to my face. You would have thought they were pure gold. That signaled that I had "arrived," in my mind. I was finally on my own with my husband. With our combined incomes, we could now afford to buy things like new towels. Then came the furniture and eventually the house. Baby steps that led to the next and then the next.

If it's guilt or bitterness or anger with someone, you can lay that aside today. The next step would be to make things right if you need to – but only if it would help. If there was another party involved, that person may have already resolved the issue in his or her mind, and your bringing it up to make you feel better may take that person back to a place he or she does not want to revisit.

Remember that actions speak louder than words. Believe me, people are going to notice the subtle changes at first when you're not carrying that guilt around. Laugh openly and freely – it really feels good. Take those baby steps to rebuilding your love of yourself. Others cannot love you as completely if you don't love yourself.

Think about what you do control, and if you're going to make a choice to change something, do it within that arena so you don't get frustrated. For instance, if you have a project you're working on and you're really not excited about it, what can you do to change that? Is the problem a person you have to spend time with on the project? Is it that the end result doesn't motivate you? Ask yourself, "How can I make this be different?" Change what you can. Either spend only the requisite time with the individual you'd rather not be with, or find a way to deal with what other byproduct of the project would make you motivated. Figure that out and take the first steps. Now you're in control, instead of being controlled.

Be Kind to Yourself

This chapter is about your turn to be happy. This can happen only if you are kind to yourself and to others. These offer different feelings of happiness. Doing for others gives you a great sense of joy, especially when you give with no thought of return. And I want to leave you with the knowledge that it is okay to take care of yourself. I know it's easier said than done. When a friend who is a psychologist first told me to take care of myself, it felt so selfish just to say it, never mind do it.

What I have since learned is that if I take care of myself, I'm an example to others to take care of themselves. Also, I realized that this did not take away from my doing for others as I had feared. Now I make sure to take time for myself with a massage here, some flowers there, little things that make me smile. You try it. Smile and enjoy life as you make those choices that can be so enriching. This is one choice that will serve you well and encourage those around you.

Take-Aways from This Chapter:

🩰 Recognize something that made you happy today. Is this something you could do more often? Determine those things that make you smile, and be sure they're in your daily life in some manner.

🩰 Make sure to take time for yourself. You won't be letting someone else down. The end result of making you feel better is that you will approach other things you have to do with a better frame of mind.

If you have a tough task to accomplish, do it first thing. If you don't, it hangs over your head all day and influences everything else. Get it done and out of your hair and you can enjoy the day. This reminds me of how I eat my meals. I save my favorite food for last. That way, the last taste is the best and what I take away with me.

Be an example. It could be at home as an example to your children, at work as a leader among your co-workers, or in the community or church as one whose actions speak louder than words.

Take a baby step today toward a goal you have made while reading this book. It doesn't matter which one, but it might help you to choose one that has a short cycle so you can see results soon. Take one step, and then another. ....

Often people attempt to live their lives backwards;
they try to have more things, or more money,
in order to do more of what they want, so they will be happier.
The way it actually works is the reverse.
You must first be who you really are,
then do what you need to do, in order to have what you want.
– Margaret Young,
1920s American singer and entertainer

Epilogue

I hope as you have taken this journey with me, you've found that of the many choices discussed, at least one touched you. On my Web site, www.cinderellaisstilldancing.com, you will find two ways in which you can share your experience:

Author's Blog: All who write to me here will find that their stories will be shared with others and that they, in turn, can respond or make comments, too.

A Private Chat with Ellen: This is a one-on-one conversation we can have that will not be shared.

My wish for you is to be happy and have a rich life, and that you share your experiences with others to help them on their journey. My own true happiness comes from the happiness of others I have touched in some way.

Resources

- www.womenshealth.gov/violence/state/ – The Violence Against Women section of the U.S. Department of Health and Human Services website.
- www.ndvh.org – The National Domestic Violence Hotline, 1-800-799-7233 (1-800-799-SAFE) or 1-800-787-3224 (TTY).
- www.nbwctucson.org – New Beginnings for Women & Children, Tucson, (520) 325-8800.
- ww5.komen.org – Susan G. Komen for the Cure, 1-877-465-6636 (1-877 GO KOMEN), or in Arizona www.komensaz.org.
- *Codependent No More: How to Stop Controlling Others and Start Caring for Yourself* by Melody Beattie.
- www.aa.org – Alcoholics Anonymous for help with substance abuse.
- www.alanon.alateen.org – Al-Anon and Alateen for people whose lives are affected by someone who abuses alcohol.

About the Author

Ellen Kirton owns and operates Tucson, Arizona-based consulting practice Consultive Business Planning. She also is the President/CFO of EffortlessHR, an internet-based company that automates human resources for small business.

Ellen has vast experience in sales and finance stemming from her 35 years in banking, the most recent having been as Senior Vice President at Chase Bank, where she ran a Small Business sector. Most of her career centered on working with small businesses. She managed staff sizes from two to 90. Ellen also helped create loan centers for a bank in California that merged 365 branches into eight loan centers statewide.

In her consulting practice, she works with small companies to build business plans, help business owners understand and use financial statements to ensure there is adequate cash flow, and obtain financing. According to one of her clients, "Ellen Kirton is extremely resourceful. She can cut through the day-to-day "fires" and help to identify the holes in a company's infrastructure."

Ellen is most proud of the relationships she builds with people, whether it is co-workers, clients, professional alliances and/or the community. She uses her expertise from her banking career and her time as a business consultant to assist community organizations she serves. She is very active in the community, having served in many positions on boards, including President of both New Beginnings for Women & Children and the Catalina Council Boy Scouts of America. Currently she is on the Executive Committees of both the Tucson chapter of National Association of Women Business Owners (NAWBO) and the Southern Arizona Affiliate of Susan G. Komen for the Cure, Ellen has also been involved in many other women's organizations, and she loves to speak to help empower women.

She has garnered many awards such as Executive Women Internationals' Woman of the Year, Member of the Year from NAWBO, and Woman of the Year from the 94.9 MIXfm radio station in Tucson, as well as much professional recognition.

Ellen KIRTON

words that sow the seeds of life

A Note About the Artist

M elo Dominguez is an experienced illustrator living in Tucson, Ariz. Her artwork is multilayered and multifaceted, as is she. Melo has the ability to interpret someone's thoughts into wonderful images to depict the very essence of the story. This is a true gift indeed.

The whole experience of working with Melo was an easy one. She focused on my goals for the book and created illustrations to match. It was a great collaboration.

Melo got her start painting murals in Los Angeles and went on to serve an internship at The Getty in Los Angeles, where she began creating art in various mediums, including watercolor, acrylic, plaster, clothing and photography. She has painted public murals and has created background sets for projects for Janet Jackson, Usher, Ralph Lauren and other high-profile clients. It has been an honor to work with her.

Melo can be reached at www.mrocla.com.